PHILOSOPHY READER:

Essays and Articles for Thought and Discussion

MAX MALIKOW, EDITOR

ISBN: 1461173787
ISBN-13: 9781461173786

To Professor Peter Kreeft: Whose teaching and writing has made philosophy comprehensible and enjoyable for a generation of students.

To Dr. Robert M. Coles: Who was investigating character education long before it became a national concern and academic curiosity.

To SC: Who has taught me much and blessed my life simply by being herself.

Philosophy Reader:
Essays and Articles for Thought and Discussion

PREFACE

This collection of essays and articles was born of dissatisfaction - first, my students' and then, my own. A few years ago, when teaching an introductory philosophy course, I was dissatisfied with the in-class discussions of the reading assignments. (There weren't any discussions!) This deficiency reflected the students' lack of interest in and enthusiasm for the textbook material. Upon realizing this, I reasoned that since all of us in the room were discontent, a change was in order.

I discontinued the textbook assignments and replaced them with less theoretical articles and essays. Although most of the replacement material was not written for a philosophy course, it was no less philosophical than the textbook it replaced. It addressed events and conditions of ordinary, everyday life. The newspaper stories, letters to the editor, excerpts from books, magazine articles, and personal correspondence that constituted "Plan - B" produced the desired result. Spirited in-class discussions followed and the idea for the anthology you are holding was conceived.

Often and justifiably, philosophers are dismissed as being so heavenly minded they're no earthly good. Philosophy at its worst is abstract, abstruse, nearly incomprehensible when read, and apparently disconnected from the issues of *real life*. Yet, when people are providing evidence for their beliefs, employing logic, making moral decisions, assessing value, and experiencing pleasure they are "doing philosophy" (Katen, 1973). Often, philosophy at its best is not immediately recognized as philosophy. If you find yourself intrigued by some of the pieces in this collection and engaged in discussions concerning them, be mindful that you are *philosophizing*.

Max Malikow
Syracuse, New York
January 27, 2011

PERMISSIONS

"An Alternate World" from *Everything Bad Is Good for You* by Steven Johnson. Used by permission of Penguin Group.

"At War with My Skin" from *Self-Consciousness* by John Updike. Used by permission of Random House, Inc.

"Feline High Rise Syndrome." from *The Power of Logical Thinking* by Marilyn vos Savante. Used by permission of the authorn given July 22, 2011.

"Intolerable Indignities" from *The Making of a Country Lawyer* by Gerry Spence. Used by permission of the author given on June 2, 2011.

"Mother Teresa's Bureaucratic Encounter" from *The Death of Common Sense* by Philip K. Howard. Used by permission of Time Warner Books.

"Of Course Priests Fall in Love" from *A Piece of My Mind ... on Just About Everything* by Andrew M. Greeley. Used by permission of Random House.

"Protecting Babies' Rights" by Alan Dershowitz. Used by permission of the author given on December 26, 2010.

"Joe Riker" from Mortal Lessons: *Notes on the Art of Surgery* by Richard Selzer. Used by permission of Harcourt, Brace, and Company.

"Sex with a Sibling" from *The Happiness Hypothesis: Finding Modern Truth in Ancient Wisdom*. Used by

INTRODUCTION

In 1907 William James articulated the challenge confronting the philosophers of his day. Conceding that "philosophy bakes no bread," he placed the onus on those professionally engaged in the discipline to make a compelling case for its usefulness (88). Such an observation was to be expected from a *pragmatist*. (One who believes the value of an idea or set of ideas resides in its practical results.)

Each of these essays and articles addresses an aspect of ordinary life. *A nurse complaining about a parking ticket. An overdue library book is returned. A college student decides to transfer to another school. Two cars, heading in opposite directions, pass each other without incident. A letter is written to a college. A man is self-conscious about a skin condition. An elderly woman's sister passes away.* At a glance, none of these mundane events merits philosophical consideration. Yet, each provides an opportunity to address one or more of seven philosophical topics: epistemology, logic, ethics, value theory, aesthetics, metaphysics, and free will/responsibility.

While the study of philosophy will never be as practical as baking bread, it is also true that "man does not live by bread alone ..." (Matthew 4:4). The purpose of this collection is to give rise to philosophical discourse, but not mere discussion for the sake of discussion. Rather, the purpose of each piece is to refine the reader's thinking on the commonplace issues that constitute real life.

Professor Ed L. Miller begins his textbook, *Questions that Matter: An Invitation to Philosophy*, with this thought:

> Philosophical reflection is not an activity indulged in only by specialists called philosophers who allegedly live in architectural monstrosities known as ivory towers. Just as each of us at times engages casually in horticulture or medicine or carpentry

without special training, so practically all of us on certain occasions spontaneously occupy ourselves with philosophical questions (1992, 1).

The essays and articles in this collection are organized under seven questions:

1. When we claim something is true, how can we be certain that it is?
2. How can we be confident that a conclusion is the result of a reliable reasoning process?
3. Are there standards and procedures for determining ethical behavior?
4. What factors make one thing more valuable than another?
5. What makes someone or something pleasing to the senses?
6. Is there reality outside of the material world that cannot be perceived by scientific investigation or the five senses?
7. Is decision-making a reality or an illusion?

A little over a century ago an eminent philosopher unambiguously stated philosophy must be practical. The pages that follow describe ordinary events not immediately recognizable as philosophical issues, but they are and thoughtful discussion of them will benefit those who engage in it.

I. Epistemology

1. <u>Introductory Thought: Why Researchers Do Not Do Well on Dates</u>

> *But man, proud man,*
> *Drest in a little brief authority,*
> *Most ignorant of what he's most assured*
> - William Shakespeare,
> *Measure for Measure*, Act II, scene 2.

Epistemology is the subcategory of philosophy concerned with the basis of human knowledge. The question pervading epistemology is: How can we be certain that anything we claim as true is in fact true? Sigmund Freud was "a convinced, consistent, aggressive atheist" (1961, xxiii). In contrast, a distinguished professor of philosophy and author of forty-seven books, Mortimer Adler, wrote: "I have reasonable grounds for affirming God's existence" (1980, 150). Two highly regarded thinkers in disagreement, each confident in the truthfulness of his assertion. Yet, at least one of them is "most ignorant of what he's most assured."

Assurance of an erroneous belief is a condition familiar to all of us. Consider that one o'clock appointment we were certain was scheduled for two o'clock. Recall that check we wrote with confidence that there was enough in the account to cover it only to have it returned stamped INSUFFICIENT FUNDS. These are but two mundane epistemological instances of certainty incompatible with reality.

Over three centuries ago Rene Descartes settled the issue of certainty to the satisfaction of many philosophers with the conclusion cogito ergo sum - "I think, therefore, I am" (2004, Part I). Descartes' noteworthy contribution notwithstanding, the assurance of our existence is rarely, if ever, a factor in the execution of our daily activities. If you doubt this, ask yourself if you have ever wondered about your existence before making an appointment or writing a check.

Five pieces are presented in this chapter, one pertains to knowledge derived from research, two address the imperfection of human knowledge, and two relate to educational issues. In keeping with the theme of this collection, all five arise from ordinary events not immediately identifiable as philosophical issues. Some involve truth claimed in spite of an insufficiency of evidence and others truth diluted by a limited perspective.

Researchers systematically gather data in order to answer a question, solve a problem, or address a significant issue. Fastidious care in making assertions is necessary in research but a hindrance in dating. In this skit, Rachel, a doctoral student conducting research, has a first date with Dave.

> Dave: I'm really sorry I was late picking you up. It's just that I always get all red lights whenever I go down Main Street.
>
> Rachel: That's not likely. If you tested that hypothesis, you'd probably see that you get as many green lights as red lights over a substantial number of trials.
>
> Also, if you really believe that you always get all red lights on Main Street then why do you drive on that street?
>
> Dave: Hmmm ... that's an interesting theory.
>
> Rachel: It's not a theory, it's a hypothesis. A hypothesis is an explanation that can be tested and either verified or falsified. A theory is an explanation or belief that cannot be tested but is logical and consistent with empirical evidence.
>
> Dave: I ... um ... never thought about Main Street that way. That's ... a ... interesting. Thanks.

Rachel: You're welcome.

Dave: This is a great restaurant.

Rachel: What is your evidence for that claim?

Dave: Well, it's crowded on a Sunday night.

Rachel: True, but there are only three restaurants in this city that are open on Sunday nights. A plausible rival hypothesis to your claim is that the crowd is the result of so few restaurant options on a Sunday night.

Dave: Well, they say it's a great restaurant.

Rachel: Who are "they?" Are "they" authorities on restaurants whose opinion should be valued? Further, how is "great" defined and by what criteria is it established?

Dave: Well, um ... I've been here before and I think it's a great restaurant.

Rachel: Now you're overgeneralizing.

Dave: "Overgeneralizing?"

Rachel: You overgeneralize whenever you say too much from too little data. Your individual experience provides an insufficient data base.

Dave: Hmmm ... I hadn't thought of that. I guess I'll have to think about it. Well, anyway, I'm happy we were able to get together tonight.

Rachel: Why does our being together tonight make you happy?

Dave: Because I think we're going to have a good time.

Rachel: How are you going to evaluate whether or not we'll have had a good time?

Dave: Well ... uh ... I'm not sure how I'll know.

Rachel: Without a methodology for analysis and evaluation you have no means for determining whether or not we'll have had a good time.

Dave: Uh ... hmmm ... I guess I'll have to think about that too. May I ask you a question?

Rachel: Yes, you may.

Dave: Every time I say something you ask me a question. Why?

Rachel: That's not true. I didn't ask you a question after you said, "May I ask you a question?" Are you claiming a cause-and-effect relationship exists between you saying something and me asking a question?

Dave: A ... yeah ... I guess I am.

Rachel: Perhaps you've noticed a correlation between you saying something and me asking a question.

Dave: What's the difference? Isn't a correlation the same thing as cause-and-effect?

Rachel: No, they're similar, but not the same. In a cause-and-effect relationship "event A" comes before "event B" and it can be demonstrated that "A" is the cause of "B." A correlation exists when two events tend to occur together, calling for further investigation.

Dave: I see ... I mean, I think I do ... ah ... thanks. Look, how about seeing a movie after dinner? The new Tom Cruise movie has gotten good reviews.

Rachel: From whom?

Dave: I knew you were going to ask me that. O.K. Some of my friends have said it's a good movie.

Rachel: But your friends do not constitute a standard random sample.

Dave: A "standard random sample?"

Rachel: Yes, a carefully constructed group that accurately represents the greater number of people it claims to represent. How can we be confident that your friends accurately speak for us unless they are a standard random sample representing you and me?

Dave: You know ... we're very different. Maybe we shouldn't date.

Rachel: What do you mean?

Dave: I mean we're different! They say ... no ... no ... I mean **I say** that "birds of a feather flock together."

Rachel: Unless that proverb originated with you, you should provide a reference. Also, for many proverbs there are equally tenable, oppositional proverbs. In this case, the proverb "opposites attract" might apply to us.

Dave: Are you saying that you want to go out on another date?

Rachel: Yes, I believe that one date is an insufficient data gathering effort.

Dave: But the way you talk drives me crazy!

Rachel: Interesting! I've had other men tell me that. I should take that claim about me seriously. Non-consulting sources that offer the same observation constitute convergent data, which has a high level of credibility.

Dave: What do you mean a "high level?" **Oh no, now you've got me doing it!**

Rachel: By "high level" I mean statistically significant – having a correlation coefficient of at least decimal point five.

Dave: Why did you say, "yes," when I asked you to go out?

Rachel: I have no reason; I just felt that I should go out with you.

Dave: You just "felt?" That doesn't sound like you. Doesn't it bother you that you have no reason for going out with me?

Rachel: Actually no ... recent neurological research on a part of the brain called the amygdala suggests that immediate cognition or intuition can be trustworthy.

Dave: Well, maybe this is the start of a special relationship after all.

Rachel: Perhaps, but since this is our first date I believe you are speaking ahead of the data.

Dave: But you are willing to have another date with me, right?

Rachel: Yes.

Dave: How about going for a ride on my motor-cycle?

Rachel: When?

Dave: Whenever you're available.

Rachel: When I asked "When?" I meant, under what conditions?

Dave: What do you mean?

Rachel: If the conditions are optimally safe then I'll go with you. According to the National Traffic Safety Council most motorcycle accidents occur in this part of the country in April on Saturday or Sunday mornings between 12:30 a.m. and 6:00 a.m. on wet pavements. If our ride will not con-form to the probability profile for motorcycle ac-cidents then I'll ride with you.

Dave: No other woman in the world would de-cide about a motorcycle ride by consulting with the National Traffic Safety Council.

Rachel: You can't say that with certainty since you haven't asked every other woman in the world to go for a ride on your motorcycle. However, you could generate a statistical statement if you asked a standard random sample representative of all women. But that would include a plus or minus factor.

Dave: I think I could live a hundred years and not meet another woman like you.

Rachel: It's unlikely you would live a hundred years. The profile of people who live to be a hundred includes female and Asian, specifically Japanese.

Dave: Rachel, I just want to go out with you.

Rachel: Why?

Dave: Because you're beautiful!

Rachel: Hmmm ...

Dave: That was a compliment! Don't you recognize a compliment when you hear one?

Rachel: Actually it's not a compliment. Beauty is largely culturally determined and a highly subjective evaluation.

Dave: I like the way you look and it makes me feel good to be with you.

Rachel: Probably it's not the way I look. More likely it's the way I smell to you.

Dave: What?

Rachel: Recent research suggests that pheromones account for how we smell to each other and contribute to romantic attraction.

Dave: Only you could use the word "romantic" in a sentence like that.

Rachel: Dave?

Dave: Oops ... I know, without a standard random sample I can't say that.

Rachel: Excellent! You're teachable. I think I'd like to go out with you again.

Dave: Why?

Rachel: Because, as I said, you're teachable. Also, you're being patient with me.

Dave: I am?

Rachel: Yes, and willingness to learn and patience correlates with the profile of the man I one day hope to marry.

Dave: **Marry!** ... uh ... now I think **you're** speaking ahead of the data! (Malikow, 2010, 8-12)

2. AN ALTERNATE WORLD

The play 12 Angry Men (Rose, 1954) takes place in one room where a dozen men deliberate on a murder case. The intensity of their interaction marks the play as aptly titled. This drama is reminiscent of the "Allegory of the Cave" found in Book VII of Plato's The Republic *(1968). In this allegory, Socrates describes the imperfect condition of human knowledge to Plato's brother, Glaucon. Socrates likens humankind to men chained from birth in a cave. Their arms and legs are shackled and their heads fixed in such a way that no movement is possible. Behind the men objects are passed in front of a fire, producing shadows on the wall in front of the men. Since each man has a different perspective from his place in the cave, no two of them see exactly the same shadow. As well, none of them see the actual object; each sees only its shadow. In this way Socrates describes the imperfection of the knowledge men claim. He adds that it is the work of philosophers to be aware of this imperfection and strive to break free from their own chains.*

The two selections that follow communicate the same concept. The first, from Steven Johnson's Everything Bad Is Good for You *(2005), describes an alternate universe in which video gaming came before reading, thereby generating parental concern about the harmful effects of reading. The second, from David Foster Wallace's celebrated Kenyon College commencement address, consists of two stories illustrating unconscious influences on our perceptions (2005).*

Imagine an alternate world identical to ours save one techno-historical change: video games were invented and popularized *before* books. In this parallel universe, kids have been playing games for centuries - and then these page-bound texts come along and suddenly they're all the rage. What would teachers, and the parents, and the cultural authorities have to say about this frenzy of reading? I suspect it would sound something like this:

Reading books chronically understimulates the senses. Unlike the longstanding tradition of gameplaying - which engages the child in a vivid, three-dimensional world filled with moving images and musical soundscapes, navigated and controlled with complex muscular movements - books are simply a barren string of words on the page. Only a small portion of the brain devoted to processing written language is activated during reading, while games engage the full range of sensory and motor cortices.

Books are also tragically isolating. While games have for many years engaged the young in complex social relationships with their peers, building and exploring worlds together, books force the child to sequester to him or herself in a quiet space, shut off from interaction with other children. These new "libraries" that have arisen in recent years to facilitate reading activities are a frightening sight: dozens of young children, normally so vivacious and socially interactive, sitting alone in cubicles, reading silently, oblivious to their peers.

Many children enjoy reading books, of course, and no doubt some of the flights of fancy conveyed by reading have their escapist merits. But for a sizable percentage of the population, books are downright discriminatory. The reading craze of recent years cruelly taunts the 10 million Americans who suffer from dyslexia - a condition that didn't even exist as a condition until printed text came along to stigmatize its sufferers.

But perhaps the most dangerous property of these books is the fact that they follow a fixed linear path. You can't control their narratives in any fashion - you simply sit back and have the story dictated to you. For those of us raised on interactive narratives, this property may seem astonishing. Why would anyone want to embark on adventure utterly choreographed by another person? But today's generation embarks on such adventures millions of times a day. This risks instilling a general passivity in our children, making them feel they're powerless to change their circumstances. Reading is not an active, participatory process; it's a submissive one. The book readers of the younger generation are learning to "follow the plot" instead of learning to lead.

3. This Is Water

David Foster Wallace's suicide in 2008 at age 46 deprived the literary world of an extraordinary talent. His novel Infinite Jest *was included on* Time's *list of the 100 best novels from 1923 to 2003.*

There are these two young fish swimming along and they happen to meet an older fish swimming the other way, who nods at them and says, "Morning, boys. How's the water?"

And the two young fish swim on for a bit, and eventually one of them looks over at the other and goes, "What the hell is water?"

... The immediate point of the fish story is merely that the most obvious, ubiquitous, important realities are often the ones that are hardest to see and talk about. Stated as an English sentence, of course, this is just a banal platitude - but the fact is that, in the day-to-day trenches of adult existence, banal platitudes can have a life-or-death importance.

... If your complete freedom of choice regarding what to think about seems too obvious to waste time talking about, I'd ask you to think about fish and water, and to bracket, for just a few minutes, your skepticism of the value of the totally obvious.

Here's another didactic little story. There are two guys sitting together in a bar in the remote Alaskan wilderness. One of the guys is religious, the other's an atheist, and they're arguing about the existence of God with that special intensity that comes after the fourth beer. And the atheist says,

> Look, it's not like I don't have actual reasons for not believing in God. It's not like I haven't experimented with the whole God-and-prayer thing. Just last month I got caught off away from the camp in that terrible blizzard, and I couldn't see a thing, and I was totally lost, and it was fifty below, and so I did, I

tried it: I fell to my knees in the snow and cried out,
"God, if there is a God, I'm lost in this blizzard, and
I'm going to die if you don't help me!"

And now, in the bar, the religious guy looks at the atheist all puzzled: "Well then, you must believe now," he says, "After all, here you are alive." The atheist rolls his eyes like the religious guy is a total simp: "No, man, all that happened was that a couple of Eskimos just happened to come wandering by, and they showed me the way back to the camp."

The nonreligious guy is so totally, obnoxiously confident in his dismissal of the possibility that the Eskimos had anything to do with his prayer for help. True, there are plenty of religious people who seem arrogantly certain of their own interpretations, too. They're probably even more repulsive than atheists, at least to most of us here, but the fact is that religious dogmatists' problem is exactly the same as the story's atheist's - arrogance, blind certainty, a close-mindedness that's like an imprisonment so complete that the prisoner doesn't even know he's locked up.

The point here is that I think this is one part of what the liberal arts mantra of "teaching me how to think" is really supposed to mean: to be just a little less arrogant, to have some "critical awareness" about myself and my certainties ... because a huge percentage of the stuff that I tend to be automatically certain of is, it turns out, totally wrong and deluded.

4. THE INDIANS OF THE SIX NATIONS TO WILLIAM & MARY COLLEGE

Educator and author Deborah Meier posits that education is more a matter of nurturing five habits of the mind than teaching a particular set of facts (1995, 79-80, 104, 107). One of these habits is questioning the relevance of what is being taught by inquiring, "How is this material useful in real-life?" Practical knowledge varies from culture to culture A letter from the Indians of the Six Nations to William & Mary College illustrates that practical knowledge varies from culture to culture. The sardonic counter-proposal made at the end of the letter challenges the presumptuousness of the college's invitation. The essay by Alfie Kohn raises at least two questions: What does it mean to be well-educated? And, what does it mean to be intelligent?

"In June 1744 ... the College of William & Mary invited the Indians of the Six Nations to send twelve young men to their college to be 'properly' educated. Soon after, William & Mary received the following reply" (Andrew Carroll, 1997, 240).

Sirs,

We know you highly esteem the kind of learning taught in Colleges, and that the Maintenance of our young Men, while with you, would be very expensive to you. We are convinc'd, therefore, that you mean to do us Good by your Proposal; and we thank you heartily. But you, who are wise, must know that different nations have different

Conceptions of things; and you will therefore not take it amiss, if our Ideas of this kind of Education happen not to be the same with yours. We have had some Experience of it. Several of our Young People were formerly brought up at the Colleges of the Northern Provinces; they were instructed in all your Sciences; but, when they came back to us, they were bad Runners, ignorant of every means of living in the Woods, unable to bear either Cold or Hunger, knew neither how to build a Cabin, take a Deer, or kill an Enemy, spoke our Language imperfectly, were therefore neither fit for Hunters, Warriors, nor Counsellors; they were totally good for nothing. We are, however, not the less oblig'd by your kind Offer, tho' we decline accepting it; and, to show our grateful Sense of it, if the Gentlemen of Virginia will send us a Dozen of their Sons, we will take care of their Education; instruct them in all we know, and make Men of them.

5. What Does It Mean to Be Well Educated?

No one should offer pronouncements about what it means to be well educated without meeting my wife. When I met Alisa, she was at Harvard, putting the finishing touches on her doctoral dissertation in anthropology. A year later, having spent her entire life in school, she decided to do the only logical thing ... and apply to medical school. Today she is a practicing physician - and an excellent one at that, judging by feedback from her patients and colleagues.

She will, however, freeze up if you ask her what eight times seven is, because she never learned the multiplication table. And forget about grammar ("Me and him went over to her house today" is fairly typical) or literature ("Who's Faulkner?"). After a dozen years, I continue to be impressed on a regular basis by the agility of her mind as well as by how much she doesn't know. (I'm also bowled over by what a wonderful person she is, but that's beside the point.)

So what do you make of this paradox with whom I live? Is she a walking indictment of the system that let her get so far - twenty-nine years of schooling, not counting medical residency - without acquiring the basics of English and math? Or does she offer an invitation to rethink what it means to be well educated since what she lacks hasn't prevented her from being a deep-thinking, high-functioning, multiply credentialed, professionally successful individual?

Of course, if those features describe what it means to be well educated, then there is no dilemma to be resolved. She fits the bill. The problem arises only if your definition includes a list of facts and skills that one must have but that she lacks. In that case, though, my wife is not alone. ... I've come to realize just how many truly brilliant people cannot spell or punctuate.

Or what about me? ... I could embarrass myself pretty quickly by listing the number of classic works of literature I've never read. And I can multiply reasonably well, but everything I was taught after first-year algebra (and even some of that) is completely gone. How well educated am I?

The issue is sufficiently complex that questions are easier to formulate than answers. So let's at least be sure we're asking the right questions and framing them well (Kohn, 2004, 1).

II. LOGIC

The truth? The truth? You can't handle the truth!

- Col. Nathan Jessup,
"A Few Good Men"

The irony in Col. Jessup's declaration is that it is the climactic exclamation of a cross-examination in which he is unmasked as a liar by his self-contradictory, illogical testimony. Each of the selections in this chapter illustrates logic by pointing to its opposite - unsound reasoning. Consider a disagreement in which you have caught your opponent in an indisputable contradiction. At the moment your opponent cannot reconcile a statement with one of his previous statements you realize you have won the argument. The principles of logic constitute the common master to whom we all are compelled to submit. If a = b and b = c then a = c for everyone. Neither can anyone refute this syllogism: All men are mortal. Socrates is a man. Therefore, Socrates is mortal.

In the following pieces a prosecution is challenged, a brilliant woman admits to faulty logic, an attorney recognizes his inconsistency, a Cambridge philosopher challenges a self-evident truth, an appealing premise results in an unpopular assertion, a faulty premise leads to an erroneous conclusion, and a parking ticket recipient makes an unconvincing, emotional plea.

The following letter to the editor appeared in the August 14, 2009 Syracuse, New York The Post Standard. *It refers to a tragic case of child abuse in which a little girl named Erin Maxwell was subjected to years of appalling neglect and repugnant living conditions. She remained in her home even after visits by social service case workers in response to numerous complaints over several years. This case received national attention when 11 year-old Erin was strangled by her step brother, 28 year-old Alan Jones, who is serving a sentence of 25 years to life.*

This letter points out the inconsistency of the court finding Erin's father and step mother guilty of child endangerment after the county social services agency allowed Erin to remain in her home.

6. DID THE JURY REACH A DECISION THAT OSWEGO CASE WORKERS DID NOT?

To the editor:

The author Susanna Kaysen says she writes "to make sense of it all." This letter is an attempt to make sense of the tragic case of Erin Maxwell.

Her father and stepmother have been found guilty of child endangerment ("subjection of a minor to an inappropriate or dangerous situation"). Why was there a trial at all? If after three visits, child protective agents determined that Erin's removal from her home was not warranted, why should Lynn and Lindsey Maxwell have suspected they were doing anything criminal? Social service professionals had declared the Maxwell home acceptable.

I am also trying to make sense of Commissioner Francis Lanigan's statement last Oct. 10: "Our role is not to go in and, you know, tear families apart. Our role is to protect the child and to secondly do what might need to be done in order to keep the family intact."

Philosopher Bertrand Russell spoke of "common sense morality." A common sense question to the commissioner and her caseworkers: Would you accept a child you love living where Erin lived?

Perhaps an indisputable definition of "unacceptable living conditions" is impossible. I am reminded of Justice Potter Stewart's words when challenged to define pornography: "I cannot define it, but I know it when I see it." I expect social workers to know "unacceptable living conditions" when they see them in extremis.

I began this letter hoping to make sense of the heartbreaking story of Erin Maxwell. I still cannot. (Malikow, 2009).

7. FELINE HIGH RISE SYNDROME

If the woman with the world's highest I.Q. can commit an error in reasoning then all of us are vulnerable to a failure of logic. Marilyn vos Savant is listed in The Guinness Book of World Records *owing to her 228 I.Q. (The genius range for I.Q. is a score of 140-145 on the Stanford-Binet Test, placing a genius in the top 25 percent of the population.) The excerpt "Falling Feline Syndrome" is from her book,* The Power of Logical Thinking *(1997).*

The New York Times weekly science supplement called "Science Times" on August 22, 1989 (stated):

> The experts have also developed startling evidence of the cat's renowned ability to survive, this time in the particular setting of New York City, where cats are prone this time of year to fall from open windows of tall buildings. Researchers call the phenomenon feline high rise syndrome.

But the side bar about how they managed to survive the falls is what interested me most.

> It elaborated " ... from June 4 through November 4, 1984, for instance, 132 such cats were admitted to the Animal Medical Center. ... Most of the cats landed on concrete. Most survived. Experts believe they were able to do so because of the laws of physics, superior balance, and what might be called the flying squirrel tactic. ...

(Veterinarians) recorded the distance of the fall for 129 of 132 cats. The falls ranged from 2 to 32 stories. ... 17 of the cats were put to sleep by their owners, in most cases not because of life-threatening injuries but because the owners said they could not afford medical treatment. Of the remaining 115, 8 died from shock and chest injuries.

Even more surprising, the longer the fall, the greater the chance of survival. Only one of 22 cats that plunged from more than seven stories died, and there was only one fracture among the 13 that fell from more than 9 stories. The cat that fell from 32 stories on concrete, Sabrina, suffered (only) a mild lung puncture and a chipped tooth.

Why did cats on higher floors fare better than those on lower ones? One explanation is that the speed of the fall does not increase beyond a certain point, (the veterinarians) said. ... This point, "terminal velocity," is reached relatively quickly in the case of cats. Terminal velocity for a cat is 60 miles per hour; for an adult human, 120 m.p.h.

Until a cat reaches terminal velocity the (veterinarians) speculated, the cat reacts to acceleration by reflexively extending its legs, making it more prone to injury. But after terminal velocity is reached, they said, the cat might relax and stretch its legs out like a flying squirrel, increasing air resistance and helping to distribute the impact more evenly.

That seemed to make sense, so I filed the article for future reference. Some time later a reader wrote to ask me to "please explain why a cat will land on its feet when it falls from a great height," and I obliged by citing the study in my column. ("Ask Marilyn," *Parade Magazine*), adding the following as an additional point of interest:

Amazingly, the cats that fell longer distances fared better than the others. Of the 22 cats that fell more than 7 stories, 21 survived; of the 13 cats that fell more than 9 stories, all survived. Sabrina, who fell 32 stories onto concrete, suffered only a minor lung puncture and a chipped tooth; I'll bet she was treated to a whole bowlful of tuna that day.

Later, reading these statistics in my published column bothered me, but I didn't know why. It never occurred to me to scrutinize the statements from the original column further. So it wasn't until my assistant dropped a handful of letters on the subject on my desk that I finally took notice. The first was from Pamela Marx in Brooklyn, New York, who wrote:

I have had two cats fall from terraces in two separate instances, and both, unfortunately, died. One was a tenth-floor terrace, and the other was on the fourteenth floor. I never reported these incidents to any medical center and believe other people probably don't report their cats deaths, either. You can add my two cats to your list and report that at least two cats died in fifteen falls over nine stories.

At that point, the error seemed so obvious that I didn't know how I had missed it in the first place.

As you know, in order to make a generalization to the population of cats falling from windows, one must be sure of having a representative sample of cats from that population. Unfortunately, using the self-selected sample of cats taken to the animal hospital after the fall in no way guarantees that. There must be many cats who fall from relatively low heights who appear unharmed to the owners, and so are not taken to the animal hospital. Similarly, there must be a number of cats who falling greater heights who die as a result and receive a shoebox funeral, also never being taken to the animal hospital. This leaves us with a biased sample of cats, not really representing the population at large.

8. Protecting Babies' Rights: Should We Let Pregnant Women Smoke and Drink?

In a 1987 newspaper article the eminent attorney and Harvard University Law School professor Alan Dershowitz admitted to a troubling conflict between two of his convictions. On one hand, on the matter of abortion he is staunchly pro-choice. On the other hand, he believes pregnant women should practice good health measures and not drink alcohol in excess, use drugs, or smoke.

The medical evidence is now overwhelming that pregnant women who smoke too much, drink too much or abuse drugs endanger the health of their babies. (So, by the way, do men who smoke in the presence of pregnant women.) No responsible person would want to bring a child into our already hazardous world with an extra preventable strike against him or her. Yet, many pregnant women and men who live with them continue to indulge in practices that are not only self-destructive but baby destructive.

A friend of mine just quit her job as a doctor in the obstetrics ward of an inner-city public hospital because she just couldn't bear another year of helping 14-year-old children (many of whom themselves had been born to 14-year-olds) give birth - prematurely - to drug-addicted or otherwise abnormal babies. She described this recurrent scene of the pregnant child with fresh needle marks, or with a cigarette hanging from her lip, or with the smell of alcohol on her breath.

The boy-father - when he came along - was often the supplier of the sickening substance to his pregnant mate. My friend tried everything - from stern lectures, to warm, sisterly advice. But except for a few cases, nothing seemed to work. Baby after baby was born with handicaps that will be difficult, if not impossible, to overcome.

"Can't the law do anything to protect the babies?" my friend asked me.

Many people believe you can pass a law to solve nearly every problem. But the law is a blunderous instrument with little capacity to make refined distinctions. "What would you have the law do?" I responded rhetorically. "Would you want to make it a crime for a pregnant woman to smoke or drink alcohol?"

My friend, who is a committed feminist as well as a caring doctor, was torn. Her pro-choice position on abortion inclined her toward resisting any government intrusion into the decisions of pregnant women. "Keep your laws off our bodies," has become a rallying cry. Any compromise with that principle might lead down the slippery slope toward requiring all pregnant women to bear their children. After all - the argument would go - if you can legislate to prevent a pregnant woman from injuring her child, why can't you legislate to prevent her from killing it?

But the reality that my friend had confronted daily seemed equally persuasive. Here are pregnant women who opted against abortion, who had decided to give birth. They all wanted healthy babies. They just needed help to keep from hurting their own offspring through impulsive acts of self-gratification. And most of them were minors themselves. It was already illegal for them to be sold alcohol, cigarettes, and, certainly, drugs.

But what about adults who are pregnant? Should they be free to act irresponsibly toward the babies they have decided to bring into the world? Should Big Brother be empowered to watch over their every move?

There are many hard questions and few easy answers. The stakes on both sides are enormous; the implications of government-monitored pregnancies are frightening. But so are the implications of allowing a laissez-faire approach to the welfare of helpless babies.

In the end, the best approach probably lies somewhere between the extremes of enacting special criminal laws for pregnant women and allowing the present catastrophic situation to continue unabated.

But that won't solve the problem. There will still be some pregnant women - children and adults - who are simply unwilling to look, or who are incapable of seeing, beyond their next drink, smoke or fix. This leads to the most difficult question: Should the law be given some limited power in extreme situations, where serious injury to the baby is a medical certainty?

In the end, both my feminist doctor friend and I remain adamantly pro-choice on the issue of abortion, and very torn on the desirability of some legislation designed to prevent abuses during pregnancy that virtually assure the birth of a handicapped baby.

The other day - as if to remind me that this was not exclusively a problem among inner-city kids - I was dining in a yuppie restaurant in Cambridge. At the next table were a husband and wife. The wife was very pregnant. Both were chain-smoking, and they were on their second bottle of wine. I watched as she gulped down the Pouilly-Fuisse and lit her dozenth Virginia Slim. Finally, I turned and said: "You're blowing smoke on me and into your baby. Could you please stop?"

She did. He didn't. They both looked at me as if I were a meddling busybody. I felt like one.

I had done the right thing. But it wasn't enough. What else can be done on behalf of these helpless babies without unduly interfering in the lives of pregnant women? (Dershowitz, 2010).

9. THE BOGUS CLAIM OF THE DECLARATION OF INDEPENDENCE

"It goes without saying" is a phrase often heard even though it contributes nothing to advancing an argument. Anything so obvious that it "goes without saying" doesn't need to be said. In Crimes Against Logic *(2004)* Jamie Whyte makes a similar observation concerning a phrase found in the* Declaration of Independence.

The boldest example of a bogus claim to obviousness is the second paragraph of the American Declaration of Independence:

> We hold these truths to be self-evident, that all men are created equal, that they are endowed by their Creator with certain unalienable Rights, that among these are Life, Liberty, and the pursuit of Happiness.

Perhaps these statements are true, perhaps not. We can't get into that here. But they are not self-evidently true.

Take the claim that all men are created equal. *Equal* must here be used with some special meaning. For it is not normally grammatical to say that things (other than numerical values) are simply equal. They must be equally something: equally tall, equally green, equally obtuse, or something. What does it mean to say simply that all people are equal? But if a statement is hard even to understand it surely cannot be self-evident.

Entitled to equal treatment under the law, or something along those lines, is probably what was meant. Yet principles of jurisprudence of this kind are debated even today. This one must have looked pretty bizarre to most reading it in 1776. Then, many Americans, including the authors of the Declaration, owned slaves. Can it really be self-evident that, in a country full of slaves, everyone is entitled to equal treatment under the law?

Candidates for self-evident truth are statements such as, "I've just fallen in a puddle" or "The tea is hot." Grand principles of justice that few have ever heard before and can hardly understand aren't really that sort of thing. It is, indeed, pretty hard to come up with any kind of evidence or support for them at all - as philosophers working in the field will tell you. Hence, the temptation to declare them self-evident (Whyte, 2004, 48).

10. THE MYTH OF MENTAL ILLNESS

Written nearly forty years ago, The Myth of Mental Illness *landed like a bomb on the playground of mental health professionals. Its author, psychiatrist Thomas Szasz, posited that since illness (or disease) only can be physical, the term "mental illness" is a misnomer. This excerpt from Dr. Szasz's book summarizes the rationale for his assertion.*

It is widely believed that mental illness is a type of disease, and that psychiatry is a branch of medicine; and yet, whereas people readily think of and call themselves "sick," they rarely think of and call themselves "mentally sick." The reason for this ... is really quite simple: a person might feel sad or elated; insignificant or grandiose; suicidal or homicidal, and so forth; he is, however, not likely to categorize himself as mentally ill or insane; that he is, is more likely to be suggested by someone else. This, then, is why bodily diseases are characteristically treated with the consent of the patient, while mental diseases are characteristically treated without his consent. (Individuals who nowadays seek private psychoanalytic or psychotherapeutic help do not, as a rule, consider themselves either "sick" or "mentally sick," but rather view their difficulties as problems in living and the help they receive as a type of counseling.) In short, while medical diagnoses are the names of genuine diseases, psychiatric diagnoses are stigmatizing labels.

1. Strictly speaking, disease or illness can affect only the body; hence, there can be no mental illness.
2. "Mental illness" is a metaphor. Minds can be "sick" only in the sense that jokes are "sick" or economies are "sick."

3. Psychiatric diagnoses are stigmatizing labels, phrased to resemble medical diagnoses and applied to persons whose behavior annoys or offends others.

4. Those who suffer from and complain of their own behavior are usually classified as "neurotic;" those whose behavior makes others suffer, and about whom others complain, are usually classified as "psychotic."

5. Mental illness is not something a person has, but it is something he does or is.

6. If there is no metal illness there can be no hospitalization, treatment, or cure for it. Of course, people may change their behavior or personality, with or without psychiatric intervention. Such intervention is nowadays called "treatment," and the change, if it proceeds in a direction approved of by society, "recovery" or "cure."

7. The introduction of psychiatric considerations into the administration of criminal law – for example, the insanity plea and verdict, diagnoses of mental incompetence to stand trial, and so forth – corrupt the law and victimize the subject on whose behalf they are ostensibly employed.

8. Personal conduct is always rule-following, strategic, and meaningful. Patterns of interpersonal and social relations may be regarded and analyzed as if they were games, the behavior of the players being governed by explicit or tacit game rules.

9. In most types of voluntary psychotherapy, the therapist tries to elucidate the implicit game rules by which the client conducts himself; and to help the client scrutinize the goals and values of the life games he plays.

10. There is no medical, moral, or legal justification for involuntary psychiatric interventions. They are crimes against humanity (Szasz, 1973, xi-xii).

11. The Unaborted Socrates

Peter Kreeft's remarkable ability to make the abstruse understandable, in lecture and print, accounts for his extraordinary popularity as a professor of philosophy at Boston College. The following excerpt from The Unaborted Socrates (1993), *is part of a hypothetical conversation in which a doctor who performs abortions is challenged by Socrates to defend the procedure. Using the teaching methodology that bears his name, Socrates engages the doctor by asking questions and insisting that the doctor defend his position without contradiction. The following dialog begins just after Herrod has conceded he does not know when in fetal development life begins.*

Socrates: Let's see. You do not know whether the fetus is a person, correct?

Herrod: Correct.

Socrates: And your work here is to kill fetuses, correct?

Herrod: Socrates, I am continually shocked by the language you choose to use. I abort unwanted pregnancies.

Socrates: By killing fetuses or by something else?

Herrod: (Sigh) By killing fetuses.

Socrates: Not knowing whether they are persons or not?

Herrod: Oh. Well ...

Socrates: You said a moment ago you did not know when the fetus became a person. Do you know now?

Herrod: No.

Socrates: Then you kill fetuses, not knowing whether they are fetuses or not?

Herrod: If you must put it that way.

Socrates: Now what would you say of a hunter who shot at a sudden movement in a bush, not knowing whether it was a deer or a fellow hunter? Would you call him wise or foolish?

Herrod: Are you saying I am a murderer?

Socrates: I am only asking one question at a time. Shall I repeat the question?

Herrod: No.

Socrates: Then will you answer it?

Herrod: (Sigh) All right. Such a hunter is foolish, Socrates.

Socrates: And why is he foolish?

Herrod: You never stop, do you?

Socrates: No. Wouldn't you say he is foolish because he claims to know what he does not know, namely, that it is only a deer and not his fellow hunter in the bush?

Herrod: I suppose so.

Socrates: Or suppose a company were to fumigate a building with a highly toxic chemical to kill some insect pests, and you were responsible for evacuating the building first. If you were unsure if there were any people left in the building and you nevertheless gave the order to fumigate the building, would that act be wise or foolish?

Herrod: Foolish, of course.

Socrates: Why? Is it not because you would be acting as if you knew something you really did not know, namely that there were no people in the building?

Herrod: Yes.

Socrates: And now you, Doctor. You kill fetuses - by whatever means, it does not matter; it may as well be a gun or a poison. And you say that you do not know whether they are human persons. Is this not to act as if you knew what you admit you do not know? And is that not folly - in fact, the height of folly, rather than wisdom?

Herrod: I suppose you want me to meekly say "Yes indeed, Socrates. Anything you say, Socrates."

Socrates: Can you defend yourself against the argument?

Herrod: No.

Socrates: It has indeed devoured you like a shark, as surely as you devour fetuses.

Herrod: I suppose you think the case is closed (Kreeft, 1993, 71-72).

12. Towing Over Parking Violation Was Excessive

In her letter to the editor that appeared in a Syracuse, New York news-paper, Rebekah Parsons argues that justice was not served when her car was towed. What is your estimate of the strength of her claim?

To the editor:

I would like to make people aware of an unfortunate event I had to endure August 31. It was a normal day for me and I had no idea there was a Syracuse University game. At 6:30 a.m. I parked on Standart Street near SU and walked to the VA Hospital, where I am a registered nurse. I was unable to move my car at 6 p.m. because it was very busy in the Intensive Care Unit where I work.

If I had left to move my car, my patient would have died. After work (7:45 p.m.), I walked to get my car and a Syracuse policeman said it was towed. I pleaded my case and the officer tried to get the towing com-pany (Syracuse Frame Service, Inc.) to let me "slide." The towing com-pany would not waive the fee. I paid $140 cash that night to retrieve my vehicle from a parking lot that was not even a mile away.

Since when does the Syracuse Police Department tow vehicles for being in violation for one hour and 45 minutes? I was not blocking a fire hydrant nor entrance into an emergency facility. I also have to pay a parking ticket of $200, which I think should be my only punishment. Since when does moving a car become more important than saving a human life? I took an oath as a medical provider and had a professional obligation. Where is the morality these days? (Parsons, 2007)

III. Ethics

13. Introductory Thought: The Sad Ending of Professor Kohlberg

Art, like morality, consists in drawing a line somewhere.
                                              - G.K. Chesterton

On January 19, 1987 a man left Massachusetts General Hospital where he was being treated for a tropical parasite he had contracted sixteen years earlier. He drove to Boston Harbor, parked his car, and committed suicide by drowning. This man was the renown Harvard psychology professor Lawrence Kohlberg, whose research on moral development is described in virtually every introductory and developmental psychology textbook published in the last twenty-five years (Kohlberg, 1984). *Was Dr. Kohlberg's final act morally wrong?* Does it matter that he had suffered both physical pain and depression since 1971 because of his illness? Does it matter that the prognosis was *the worst is yet to come*?

This chapter is concerned with ethical conduct. The playwright and novelist Oscar Wilde is credited with having defined a *dilemma* as a situation in which "no matter what you choose, you're wrong." While this is an agreeable characterization of a dilemma, most ethical challenges are not dilemmas. In *Why Johnny Can't Tell Right from Wrong*, psychology professor William Kirk Kilpatrick argues that moral dilemmas are poor illustrations for ethical instruction because most moral decision-making requires choosing between options that are obviously right and wrong (1993). He posits that ethical conduct rarely involves a conundrum but almost always requires courage. Of the eight articles in this chapter, only one ("The Pillow Angel Debate") can be characterized as a moral dilemma. But all are controversial and, therefore, worthy of discussion.

14. BOOK OVERDUE 60 YEARS, HE PAYS UP TO MAKE POINT

Normally, the return of an overdue library book is not a newsworthy event. However, when 69 year old William Vassily returned a book he had checked out when he was 9 years old, he provided an example of integrity as well as gratitude.

William Vassily could have put his overdue book in an envelope and sent it back to the public library in Portland, Maine. That wasn't enough, he said. The book, *The Baby Whale, Sharp Ears*, was written by John Y. Beaty and published in 1938. Vassily checked it out of the library in 1946, when he was 9 years old and living in Portland, Maine. Now he lives in Clay.

That made the book 22,008 days overdue when Vassily finally returned it Friday, along with late charges of $440.16.

"My motivation for returning the book, and especially for paying the fine, is my way of giving back to the city of Portland and the Portland Public Library," Vassily said.

The fine for overdue books was 2 cents a day in 1946. So, Vassily, 69, calculated the number of days the book was late to come up with how much he owed. Vassily said the book was accidentally packed away 60 years ago, when his family moved from Portland to New York. Vassily actually didn't owe the amount he paid. Fines for late children's books in Portland are capped at $10 per item.

He hopes the news of his paying the fine in full will provide publicity and motivate people to use the library.

"The library is a door to the rest of the world for any kid or adult who wants to take advantage of it," Vassily said.

The book, about the adventures of a baby sperm whale, is out of print. It's now on display at the Portland library, along with Vassily's library card, which expired in 1947 (Leo, 2006).

15. Don't Be So Fast to Condemn Bank Robbery

On October 20, 2009 a former high school math teacher was sentenced to four years in prison following a guilty plea for a bank robbery. Six months earlier Mark Gurniak, armed with a shotgun, held up an East Syracuse, New York bank. Gurniak, age twenty-eight, said he was in desperate need of money due to gambling debts. Soon after the robbery and prior to Gurniak's plea and sentencing, this letter to the editor appeared in the The Post Standard *(Syracuse, New York).*

To the Editor:

In his letter May 21, Dave Armstrong expresses strong feelings about the high school teacher who allegedly robbed the bank.

I think the term is "innocent until proven guilty." Mark Gurniak has yet to be convicted, and funnier things have happened during a trial.

You say having money issues doesn't give you the right to rob a bank. This man obviously felt like he had no other option - if he really did do it. I have three kids and a wife and I would do anything to make sure they were OK. In this world there is no person who will help you and yours but you.

You have no place being the judge and jury in a situation that you know almost nothing about. You say that now his child and wife have to visit him in prison. In the end I would rather have my kids able to say that when they were in dire straits their father did what he had to do and I can look him in the eye because he didn't back away.

I am not condoning robbery, just saying every person will react differently, given dire situations. He is no different (Skrocki, 2009).

16. Is It Possible to Be Pathologically Good?

But I could have told you Vincent, this world
was never meant for one as beautiful as you.

- Don McLean

Common wisdom teaches *anything too good to be true isn't*, but the same cannot be said about anything *too bad*. When Richard Kuklinski was asked how many murders he had committed, "The Ice Man" hesitated before settling on an estimate of 230. This astonishing number and Kuklinski's reflection that he killed without a tinge of emotion mark him as pathologically bad, if not evil. If it is possible to be pathologically bad, is it also possible to be pathologically good? In this treatise Zell Kravinsky, Simone Weil, and Albert Schweitzer are considered to pursue the possibility of benevolent behavior so extreme that it indicates a mental illness.

The American Psychiatric Association's *Diagnostic and Statistical Manual* does not have the category *pathological altruism* or anything resembling it. Nevertheless, can altruism be expressed to a degree that it is symptomatic of a psychological disorder rather than an expression of sheer human decency? Perhaps interest in the possibility that extreme kindness suggests a mental illness arises from an internal conflict. On one hand we believe our lives to be our own and are entitled to live for ourselves. Simultaneously, a voice within speaks to us about the needs of others and our obligation to them. That voice informs us that the resources we enjoy spending on self-gratification come from grace (unmerited favor) and constitute the test of which Mother Teresa spoke when she posited we are indebted to the poor because they provide us with an opportunity to prove we are as charitable as we claim. In Nick

Hornby's novel, *How to Be Good*, a wife finds her husband's extreme kindness so discomforting she contemplates divorcing him (2001).

A century ago William James expressed his conviction that philosophy's great challenge was to refute the assertion of its detractors who claimed since "philosophy bakes no bread" it is a frivolous discipline (1907, 83). A century later, Timothy Luke Johnson asserted the purpose of studying philosophy is not to "think well" but to "live well" (2007). How will an answer to the question of the possibility of pathological goodness buttress James' conviction that engagement in philosophy is a pragmatic endeavor and support Johnson's belief that philosophy's *raison d'etre* is to contribute to living well? The answer is the issues of charity and self-sacrifice can generate guilt if the questions *how much charity* and *how much sacrifice* are unanswered. Any effort to mitigate guilt and contribute to living well is as practical as baking bread. Out of this conviction the possibility of *pathological goodness* is worthy of consideration.

Zell Kravinsky

Zell Kravinski once sought goodness through prayer. "I used to pray to God to be good. I used to fantasize about a pill that I could take that would make me good. Then I realized it's putting the cart before the horse. First, you do the good deed" (Fagone, 2006). In the wake of his existential epiphany it is indisputable that Kravinsky has sought goodness through charity. He has donated a kidney to a stranger and expressed a willingness to donate the one remaining. "What if someone needed it who could produce more good than me?" (Strom, 2003). Kravinsky believes, "To withhold a kidney from someone who would otherwise die means valuing one's own life at 4,000 times that of a stranger" (Singer, 2006). He arrived at that figure from the survivor ratio of donors who undergo the procedure (4,000 to 1). It cannot be said that were he better educated he would not be so organically philanthropic. He has earned two Ph.D.'s, one in rhetoric and a second in English literature, and nearly accomplished a third in cultural anthropology.

To say Kravinsky lives charitably is an understatement. He has donated $45,000,000 to various causes, including the largest donation ever made to the Centers for Disease Control ($6.2 million dollars). It cannot be said that Kravinsky should see a mental health professional. He lives with one, his wife Emily is a psychiatrist. Notwithstanding, a family friend offered this observation of Kravinsky's benevolent actions: "Sometimes there's a slightly pathological element to them" (Singer, 2006). Paul Find, Professor of Psychiatry at Temple University, opined: "If he does (make a second kidney donation) then there's something really wrong. And, if I was his wife, I'd have him committed" (Singer, 2006). And if altruism's most vehement critic, the philosopher and novelist Ayn Rand, had known Zell Kravinski, she would have challenged his philosophy, if not his sanity:

> If a man accepts the ethics of altruism, he suffers the following consequences (in proportion to the degree of his acceptance): (1) Lack of self-esteem - since his first concern in the realm of values is not how to live his life, but how to sacrifice it. (2) Lack of respect for others - since he regards mankind as a herd of doomed beggars crying for someone's help (1961, 49).

Is Zell Kravinsky pathologically benevolent? The renown psychiatrist Thomas Szasz would say *no*. In *The Myth of Mental Illness* he posited that behaviors cannot be "sick."

> Strictly speaking, disease or illness can only affect the body; hence, there can be no mental illness. "Mental illness" is a metaphor. Minds can be "sick" only in the sense that jokes are "sick" or economies are "sick" (1973, 267).

Dr. Szasz has long maintained that when individuals are diagnosed as mentally ill solely on the basis of their behavior the diagnosis cannot be justified. He believes the absence of a standard of human behavior makes it impossible to speak of any behavior as "sick." While he agrees that behavior is criminal when it is not in conformity to the law, he does not believe any illegal behavior constitutes a mental illness. In *The*

Second Sin he dismisses the concept of "not guilty by reason of mental defect:"

> Psychiatric expert testimony (is) mendacity masquerading as medicine (1973, 40). ... There can be no humane penology so long as punishment masquerades as "correction." No person or group has the right to correct a human being; only God does (42-43).

Szasz, who eschews most psychiatric labels, would be quick to point out mental health professionals do not include *pathological benevolence* or anything approximating it among their 415 psychiatric conditions. In contrast, the DSM - IV includes personality disorders that imply an individual's *pathological badness* toward others (antisocial personality disorder, borderline personality disorder, and narcissistic personality disorder).

G.K. Chesterton observed, "Art, like morality, requires drawing a line someplace" (2010, 839). Line drawing also applies to distinguishing normal from abnormal behavior, but who decides where to place this line and how this decision should be made? Why is the benevolence of Albert Schweitzer and Mother Teresa worthy of a Nobel prize and Zell Kravinski's altruism indicative of a mental illness? To be consistent, his mental health cannot be questioned without also questioning the psychological well-being of Jesus Christ who taught, "Greater love has no one than this, that he lay down his life for his friends" and then proceeded to do exactly that (John 15:13). Kravinsky maintains, "The only cure for the disease of wealth is to spend money" (Singer, 2006). This view is reminiscent of Jesus' instruction to the wealthy man who asked: "Good teacher, what must I do to inherit eternal life" (Luke 18:18)? Jesus responded, "Sell everything you have and give to the poor, and you will have treasure in heaven. Then come follow me" (Luke 18:22). Unlike that rich man, Zell Kravinsky has divested himself of his wealth.

Why does Zell Kravinsky's sacrificial benevolence raise a suspicion of psychological disorder while the extraordinary altruism of Mother Teresa is deemed worthy of candidacy for sainthood? Perhaps it is because mundane kindness is easily recognized and appreciated as simple human decency and the sacrificial calling of Mother Teresa has the endorsement of a religious order and Nobel committee. In contrast, Kravinsky's unique altruism is relatively unknown, having been publicized only in feature stories characterizing his generosity as eccentric, if not bizarre. Perhaps it is his self-orchestrated, self-destruction that provokes dubiety concerning his mental health. The eminent psychologist Kay Jamison's opening pages of her memoir, *An Unquiet Mind*, describe a heroic jet pilot's decision to stay with his failing plane in order to guide it away from a schoolyard full of children at play and into a mountainside where it crashed and exploded. Years later, Jamison reflected:

> Over the next few days (after the crash) it became clear from the release of the young pilot's final message to the control tower before he died, that he knew he could save his own life by bailing out. He also knew, however, that by doing so he risked that his unaccompanied plane would fall onto the playground and kill those of us who were there.
>
> The dead pilot became a hero, transformed into a scorchingly vivid, completely impossible ideal for what was meant by the concept of duty. ... The memory of the crash came back to me many times over the years, as a reminder both of how one aspires after and needs such ideals, and of how killingly difficult it is to achieve them (1995, 12-13).

In circumstances not of his making the pilot chose the lives of others over his own and died in the line of duty. In contrast, Kravinsky is seeking out opportunities for distributing his assets and, if he could have his way, sacrificing his health and quality of life. He rationalizes this with a utilitarian argument: "No one should have a second car until everyone has one. And no one should have two kidneys until everyone has one" (Strom, 2003). However, the guiding principle of utilitarianism is not simply *the greatest good for the most number* but *the greatest good for the most number of involved parties*. Kravinsky's charity to unknown others is at the expense of those known to him - his wife and children. In *Civilization and Its Discontents*, Sigmund Freud postulated indiscriminate love is a love of little worth:

> ... readiness for a universal love of mankind and the world represents the highest standpoint which man can reach. ... I should like to bring forward my two main objections to this view. A love that does not discriminate seems to me to forfeit a part of its own value, by doing an injustice to its own object; and secondly, not all men are worthy of love (1989, 66).

Simone Weil

Simone Weil is as difficult to classify as she is to characterize. Three-quarters of a century after her death she is variously referred to as a philosopher, social activist, philanthropist, Marxist, religious seeker, and Christian mystic. T.S. Eliot remembered her as "a woman of genius, of a kind of genius akin to that of saints" (Liukkonen, 2010). Born in 1909 into a privileged family in Paris, she mastered Greek by age twelve and Sanskrit shortly thereafter as part of her unrelenting determination to study and understand the world she inhabited. Weil placed first in the entrance examination to the prestigious Ecole Normal Superieure in Paris. (Another embryonic genius, Simone de Beavior, who would later distinguish herself as an existential philosopher and metaphysical novelist, placed second.)

Weil displayed uncommon sensitivity to the plight of others as early as age six when she refused sugar in sympathy with French soldiers fighting on the Western Front in World War I. At sixteen she identified with the working class and declared herself a Bolshevist and trade unionist. She frequently shared her salary with the unemployed. In 1934, in spite of her frail health, she took a leave of absence from teaching philosophy to work in a factory to intensify her protest of the exploitation of laborers. Weil disdained the ivory tower refuge of the academy, believing a life isolated from manual labor and its suffering would disable her for meaningful teaching and writing. In this vein she wrote: "The intelligent man who is proud of his intelligence is like the condemned man who is proud of his cell" (Liukkonen, 2010). Her death at age thirty-four was attributed to a combination of tuberculosis, refusal of medical treatment, and physical neglect that included periods of starvation during political protests.

Her spiritual journey accelerated six years before her death when in Italy in the same church in which Saint Francis of Assisi prayed, she had a spiritual encounter. This experience had the life-changing effect described by William James in *The Varieties of Religious Experience* (1902). Previous to her epiphany, Weil's world view was secular and agnostic, if not atheistic. Following this experience, she measured life from a sacred, theological perspective.

This radical reorientation fit James' characterization of an authentic religious conversion as an experience originating outside of the individual. He maintained religious conversions are not a mere reworking of ideas already held. If such were the case, the experience simply would be an intellectual exercise. Rather, the psychology of religious conversion requires the introduction and embracing of ideas totally foreign to the one receiving them.

Mother Teresa's calling occurred in the context of a religious tradition (Roman Catholic) that includes the possibility of personal direction from revelation (calling). A purely psychological interpretation of Weil's conversion might explain it as the culmination of her frustration with the ineffectiveness of social and political institutions in significantly alleviating human suffering. Her conclusion, "From human beings, no help can be expected," implies her disillusionment with Marxism and suggests her realization that a radically different means for change was required (Liuukonen, 2010).

In David Foster Wallace's insightful meditation, *This Is Water*, he speaks of the unconscious error of incorrectly explaining phenomena in terms of existing presuppositions when the correct explanation might require reconsidering a previously rejected possibility (2009). Perhaps the explanation for Simone Weil's conversion is not secular and psychological but is to be found in the world view she once dismissed. Perhaps, like Mother Teresa, she heard a voice from the spiritual realm that had the effect of redirecting her. It may have been the same voice heard by Albert Schweitzer.

Albert Schweitzer

Just as Mother Teresa has served a generation of baby-boomers as a paradigm of self-sacrificial human service, Albert Schweitzer did the same for the previous generation. The son of a Lutheran pastor, he distinguished himself throughout Europe as a musician and theological scholar by age twenty-eight. In 1896 he reflected on what he considered his life of privilege and made a decision about his future.

> One brilliant summer morning at Gunsbach, during the Whitsuntide holidays - it was in 1896 - as I awoke, the thought came to me that I must not accept this good fortune as a matter of course, but must give something in return. ... What the character of my future activities would be was not yet clear to me. I left it to chance to guide me. Only one thing was certain, that it must be direct human service, however inconspicuous its sphere (Schweitzer, 1933, 82).

"From everyone who has been given much, much will be demanded; and from the one who has been entrusted with much, much more will be asked" (Luke 12:48). With these words Jesus commissioned his disciples. Schweitzer's gratitude for what he had received accounts for his resolution to spend the balance of his life giving. After committing himself to hands-on human service he became aware of the need for a physician in equatorial Africa. Upon learning of this need, he entered medical school at the University of Strasbourg in 1905 and graduated in 1912. He explained his determination to serve as a physician in terms of its contrast to his life as a scholar: "I wanted to be a doctor that I might be able to work without having to talk because for years I have been giving myself out in words (1933, 82)."

Dr. Schweitzer's compassion and reverence for life encompassed all living things. He believed, "A man is truly ethical only when he obeys the compulsion to help all life he is able to assist, and shrinks from injuring anything that lives" (1933, 235). An adherent to the Hindu principle of "nonviolence to all living things" (*ahimsa*), he admitted to ambivalence when choosing human life over that of a virus or tumor, for even they are life forms.

> I rejoice over the new remedies for sleeping sickness, which enable me to preserve life, where once I could only witness the progress of a painful disease. But every time I put the germs that cause the disease under the microscope I cannot but reflect that I have to sacrifice this life in order to save another. ... every day the responsibility to sacrifice one life for another caused me pain. Standing, as all living beings are, before this dilemma of the will to live, man is constantly forced to preserve his life and life in general only at the cost of other life. If he has been touched by the ethic of Reverence for Life, he injures and destroys life only under a necessity he cannot avoid, and never from thoughtlessness (1933, 236).

Does Schweitzer's philosophical consistency constitute an obsession with life worthy of designation as a mental illness? He performed surgery neither annoyed nor distracted by flies flitting about the operating room. Rare? Yes. Extreme? Of course. Sick? If so, why? Dr. Szasz would insist the absence of a universal understanding of how people *ought* to behave means Schweitzer is unlike most people and even eccentric, but not mentally ill. Freud, were he aware of Schweitzer's unrestricted admiration for life, would question his philosophy if not his mental health. As previously stated, "A love that does not discriminate ... (forfeits) a part of its own value, by doing an injustice to its object ..." (1989, p. 66).

The Question

This essay began with a question: *Is it possible to be pathologically good?* Alternatively stated, *is there a degree of benevolence that can be explained only as a manifestation of mental illness?* To this point, Zell Kravinsky, Simone Weil, and Albert Schweitzer have been considered. Each is renown for a life of altruism. On what basis might it be concluded that the noteworthy life of any or all of them is attributable to a psychological disorder?

The altruistic lives of these individuals, while extraordinary, are not identical. The sacrifices of Kravinsky and Schweitzer provided benefits for others. The same cannot be said of Weil's self-denial. Except for the few unemployed recipients of Weil's money and those students who may have been inspired by her compassion, her lifestyle provided no tangible advantage for others. Further, her asceticism deprived her family of a daughter and sister. Weil's neglect of her well-being is reminiscent of Dostoevsky's Lise in *The Brothers Karamazov*:

> ... (Lise) unlocked the door, opened it a little, put her finger in the crack, and slammed the door as hard as she could. Ten seconds later she released her hand, went slowly to the chair, sat down, and looked intently at her blackened, swollen finger and the blood that was oozing out from under the nail. Her lip quivered.

> "I'm a vile, vile, vile, despicable creature," she whispered. (1970, 703).

Like Lise, Weil's self-inflicted suffering had no effect beyond herself. Zell Kravinsky also gave at the expense of his family. In addition to depriving his wife and children of great wealth, he was prepared to deprive his family of a husband and father. (The question of whether millions of dollars would have provided a better life for them is not at issue. The reality is that he decided to remove this advantage from his family and distribute it to others.) Only Schweitzer's benevolence came at no cost to his family.

In contrast to the quasi-martyrdom of Kravinsky and Weil, Schweitzer committed himself to living for others and served fifty-two years in Africa. Even Ayn Rand would have recognized this difference and characterized Kravinsky and Weil as concerned with how to die rather than how to live (1961, 49).

Since *pathological goodness* is not to be found in the DSM - IV, extreme altruism technically cannot be a mental illness. Further, as Dr. Szasz correctly maintains, there is no universally accepted standard for human behavior. Hence, there is no line to be drawn between laudable and pathological benevolence. However, the differences between the altruism of Albert Schweitzer and that of Zell Kravinsky and Simone Weil cannot be disregarded. This is not to declare Kravinsky and Weil mentally ill. It is to say that their benevolence is enigmatic. Perhaps the explanation for the suspiciousness of their extreme goodness is their failure to convince others of their calling. Concerning such persuasion, in *The Second Sin* Szasz wrote:

> If we can define and experience our desire as our duty - then our happiness or our lack of it shall depend on whether we can persuade others that such is the case. In proportion as we succeed in persuading them, we can become accredited as moral leaders: Tolstoy and Gandhi were eminently successful at this. In proportion as we fail in persuading them, we become defined as mad fanatics (1973, 48).

(Malikow, 2010).

17. SEX WITH A SIBLING

This moral dilemma, created by psychologist Jonathan Haidt, provides an opportunity to consider the basis upon which certain behaviors are considered immoral.

Julie and Mark are brother and sister. They are traveling together in France on summer vacation from college. One night they are staying alone in a cabin near the beach. They decide that it would be interesting and fun if they tried making love. At the very least, it would be a new experience for each of them. Julie was already taking birth control pills, but Mark uses a condom too, just to be safe. They both enjoy making love, but they decide to never do it again. They keep that night as a special secret, which makes them feel even closer to each other. What do you think about that? Was it ok for them to make love? (Haidt, 2006, 20-21).

18. The Closing of the American Mind

Rarely does a philosophy book enjoy bestseller status, let alone a place at the top of the bestseller list. But in 1987 University of Chicago philosophy professor Alan Bloom wrote The Closing of the American Mind, *hailed in* The New York Times Book Review *as: "An unparalleled reflection on today's intellectual and moral climate ... a genuinely profound book."*

After reading this excerpt, consider whether Professor Bloom's observation is dated or descriptive of today's college students.

There is one thing a professor can be absolutely certain of: almost every student entering the university believes, or says he believes, that truth is relative. If this belief is put to the test, one can count on the students' reaction: they will be uncomprehending. That anyone should regard the proposition as not self-evident astonishes them, as though you were calling into question $2 + 2 = 4$. These are things you don't think about. The students' backgrounds are as various as America can provide. Some are religious, some are atheists; some are to the Left, some to the Right; some intend to be scientists, some humanists or professionals or businessmen; some are poor, some rich. They are unified only in their relativism and their allegiance to equality. And the two are related in a moral intention. The relativity of truth is not a theoretical insight but a moral postulate, the condition of a free society, or so they see it. They have all been equipped with this framework early on, and it is the modern replacement for the inalienable natural rights that used to be the traditional American grounds for a free society. That it is a moral issue for students is revealed by the character of their response when challenged - a combination of disbelief and indignation: "Are you an absolutist?," the only alternative they know, uttered in the same tone as, "Are you a monarchist?" or "Do you really believe in witches?" This latter leads into the indignation, for someone who believes in witches might well be a witch-hunter or a Salem judge. The danger they have been taught to fear from absolutism is not error but intolerance. Relativism is necessary to openness; and this is the virtue, the only virtue, which all primary education for more than fifty years has dedicated itself to inculcating. Openness - and the relativism that makes it the only plausible stance in the face of various claims to truth and various ways of life and kinds of human beings - is the great insight of our times. The true believer is the real danger. The study of history and of culture teaches that all the world was mad in the past; men always thought they were right, and that led to wars, persecutions, slavery, xenophobia, racism, and chauvinism. The point is not to correct the mistakes and really be right; rather it is not to think you are right at all.

The students, of course, cannot defend their opinion. It is something with which they have been indoctrinated. The best they can do is point out all the opinions and cultures there are and have been. What right, they ask, do I or anyone else have to say one is better than the others? If I pose the routine questions designed to refute them and make them think, such as, "If you had been a British administrator in India, would you have let the natives under your governance burn the widow at the funeral of a man who had died?," they either remain silent or reply that the British should never have been there in the first place. It is not that they know very much about other nations, or their own. The purpose of their education is not to make them scholars but to provide them with a moral virtue - openness (Bloom, 1987, 1).

19. THE NECESSITY OF LYING

That lying is a necessity of life is itself a part of the problematic character of existence.

- Friedrich Nietzsche

Truthfulness in statements ... is the formal duty of an individual to everyone, however great may be the disadvantage according to himself or to another.

- Immanuel Kant

The final scene in "The Godfather: Part I" portrays Michael Corleone lying to his wife, Kay, after she asked him if he killed their brother-in-law, Carlo. Unable to dissuade her questioning by reminding her of their understanding that she would never ask about his business affairs, he relents and lies to her with a one-word denial: "No." The scene and movie end with a greatly relieved Kay embracing Michael, not doubting that she has heard the truth and unaware that the stage has been set for "The Godfather: Part II."

This essay addresses the phenomenon of lying. Stated as a question, this piece asks: *Is it always morally wrong to lie or is lying something we all must inevitably do in order to effectively manage life?* Before proceeding, a definition of *lie* is required. As a noun, a lie *is a false statement or piece of information deliberately presented as a falsehood.* As a verb, lying is *to present information with the intention of deceiving; to convey a false image or impression* (*American Heritage Dictionary*, 1973, 754).

Noteworthy is that lying is *not* one of the seven deadly sins (pride, envy, anger, sloth, avarice, gluttony, and lust). Neither is lying's antithesis, truth-telling, listed among the four cardinal virtues (temperance, fortitude, justice, and prudence). Still, it could be argued that telling the truth often requires courage (fortitude), fairness (justice), and wisdom (prudence). It cannot be taken lightly that most parents instruct their children to be unswervingly honest with injunctions like, "No matter what you've done, always tell us the truth." Few, if any, children have been instructed to tell the truth selectively or lie judiciously.

Tolerable Lies

There is almost unanimous agreement among philosophers that "the complicated nature of human affairs" requires sporadic, intentional deception (Martin, 1995, 70). Immanuel Kant is a conspicuous exception. "Unlike most of his followers, he believed there is an *absolute* (exceptionless) duty never to lie" (64). An oft employed hypothetical scenario supporting the majority view is the hiding of Jews in Nazi era Germany. It's absurd to think a rescuer harboring Jews would answer honestly if asked by a Gestapo officer, "Are you hiding Jews?" Parents routinely insist that their children misrepresent the truth when they are told to express appreciation for a Christmas gift from grandma, even if it is something they neither want nor like. In a magazine essay, "Liar, Liar, Parents on Fire," Katherine Deveny describes lying to her daughter:

> When my daughter asked me why it was em-
> barrassing that former New York governor Eliot
> Spitzer was involved with a cowgirl ring, I didn't
> hesitate. "Bad lariat tricks," I explained.
>
> She looked a little confused, but I let it drop. I know
> that I'm not supposed to lie to my kid, but I didn't
> feel like explaining prostitution to a 7-year old. But
> it is hardly the first whopper I've told my child, and
> it got me thinking about how I really feel about
> honesty as a policy (*Newsweek*, 04/07/08).

After considering the matter, Deveny concluded,

> I'm going to try to stop lying to my daughter be-
> cause I want her to trust me, and because I don't

want her to learn that lying is an effective strate-
gy for dealing with the adult world. Even if that's
the sad truth (04/07/08).

Is it a sad truth that lying is a necessary evil? Further, are there situations in which lying might be considered a noble act even if the term
honorable lies has an oxymoronic tone? It seems another sad truth
is that conflicts between virtues occur. Lawrence Kohlberg's *moral
stages theory*, found in virtually every introductory psychology textbook, includes *stage four* (rules and laws should be obeyed) and *stage
five* (sometimes rules and laws must be suspended to serve a greater
good) (1984). Lying or in some other way deceiving the Gestapo in
its search for Jews would be a stage five instantiation and as well as
an honorable lie. Similarly, when Senator John McCain was a prisoner of war, he gave his interrogators the names of the Green Bay
Packers' offensive line when asked for the names of the men in his
squadron.

It has been said that a dilemma is a situation in which no matter what
you choose, you'll be wrong. Although dilemmas are capable of generating spirited discussion, psychologist William Kirk Kilpatrick believes
they should not be used in moral education. In *Why Johnny Can't Tell
Right from Wrong*, he explains why dilemmas are counterproductive for
teaching ethics:

> The question to ask about this admittedly stimu-
> lating approach is this: Do we want to concen-
> trate on quandaries or on everyday morality? ...
> A great deal of a child's moral life - or an adult's
> for that matter - is not made up of dilemmas at
> all. Most of our "moral decisions" have to do with
> temptations to do things we know we shouldn't
> do or temptations to avoid doing the things we
> know we should do. ... The danger on focusing
> on problematic dilemmas such as these is that a
> student may begin to think that all of morality is
> similarly problematic (1992, 84-85).

Lying to save people from a concentration camp, protect grandma's feelings, withhold confusing information from a child, and shield comrades have something in common. In each of these instances the lie is for the benefit of someone other than the liar. If there is such a thing as honorable lying, it is done in the service of others. Dr. Benjamin Carson, a noted pediatric neurosurgeon, recounts this deception by which he and his brother were served favorably:

> My mother was a domestic. Through her work, she observed that successful people spent a lot more time reading than they did watching television. She announced that my brother and I ... had to read two books each (every week) ... and submit to her written book reports. She would mark them up with check marks and highlights. Years later we realized her marks were a ruse. My mother was illiterate; she had only received a third grade education (2006, 28-29).

However, this is not to say that *any* lie that provides a benefit to someone other than the liar is noble. The benefit of the deception must be substantial to the one being deceived - a judgment often not easily made. A husband might choose to withhold from his wife that he has committed adultery knowing she would be devastated to learn of his betrayal. However, not knowing of his infidelity mitigates her exercise of free will since she will not have the opportunity to decide if she wants to be married to a man who has been unfaithful. The obvious benefit of nondisclosure for him would be avoidance of considerable discomfort and embarrassment.

It is possible for a lie to serve the interest of the liar, put the recipient at a disadvantage, yet still be tolerable. In football games quarterbacks deceive the defense by faking passes on running plays. In poker, bluffing is a deceptive maneuver by which a player bets heavily on a poor hand or lightly on a good one. It seems odd to refer to these activities as lying since they are understood by the participants as part of the contest. Nevertheless, play-faking and bluffing are strategic deceptions.

An especially interesting type of lie is one that the recipient assumes to be a misrepresentation of the truth. Interrogating police officers and cross examining attorneys often assume they are being lied to and account for this in their questioning. In fact, one of the reasons for the courts exempting husbands and wives from testifying against their spouses is the temptation to give false testimony would be close to irresistable. Attempts to deceive police officers and juries are hardly morally right, but they are understood as highly probable.

Lying as a Necessary Evil

Since lying includes all forms of intentional deception, it is appropriate to turn attention to misrepresentations in scientific research. Stanley Milgram's *Obedience and Compliance Experiment* is one of psychology's best known investigations (1974). Less well-known, but equally intriguing, is David Rosenhan's "Sane in an Insane Place" study (1973). These renown studies could not have been accomplished without intentional misrepresentations to the subjects. Numerous other studies involve placebos, inert substances that have no medicinal power. Integral to the placebo effect is the subjects' belief that they are receiving an actual drug. These deceptions, like play-action fakes in football and bluffing in poker, are rarely thought of as lies. Still, all of them have the common characteristic of withholding the truth. The moral question raised by these practices is one of *cost-benefit analysis* in which the cost of an ethical compromise is weighed against the benefit of some accomplishment.

Figures of speech that combine seemingly contradictory expressions not only add zest to discourse but also imply something about the complexity of life. The oxymoron *necessary evil* communicates that some worthy goal can be reached only by resorting to wrongdoing. (One of the airplanes involved in the atomic bombing of Hiroshima in World War II was named "Necessary Evil.") Driving well above the speed limit and slowing down, but not stopping, at intersections is defensible conduct when rushing an injured child to the emergency room. An honest assessment of some situations would force most people to the conclusion that there are circumstances in which wrongdoing is justifiable.

As previously stated, Immanuel Kant has offered the minority opinion that lying is always morally wrong and should never be employed. "Kant was a duty ethicist, that is, someone who defines right acts as those required by duty. Unlike most of his followers, he believed there is an *absolute* - life - referred to by Kant as a *categorical imperative*. (Reconsider the example of hiding Jews and being questioned by the Gestapo.) Telling the truth at the expense of someone's life fits the description "exceptionless duty never to lie" (Martin, 1989, 57). However, Kant himself would have encountered conflicting ethical imperatives if his duty to always tell the truth would have resulted in someone's death. Truth-telling in such an instance would be contrary to the fundamental duty to respect human life and could be characterized by the wry aphorism, "The operation was a success, but the patient died."

Why Is Lying Unethical?

Perhaps this seems an odd question, given that everybody knows that *honesty is the best policy*. This is precisely what psychologists Martin Seligman and Chris Peterson found in their investigation of universal virtues (2004). Honesty was one of twenty-four *signature strengths*, also referred to as *ubiquitous virtues*, identified in their study of virtues affirmed by all cultures regardless of when or where they exist or have existed.

A biblical condemnation of lying is implied in the Ten Commandments: "Thou shalt not bear false witness against thy neighbor" (Deuteronomy 5:20). Divine disapproval of lying is emphatically reinforced in the New Testament where God strikes dead Ananias and Sapphira for lying (Acts 5: 1-11).

The stereotypical used car salesman who makes car buyers thankful for CARFAX (vehicle history reports) and the "lemon law" (the buyer's right to return a dysfunctional car) has acted unethically when his misrepresentation hinders a prospective buyer's free will decision-making. Unavoidable unknowns make used car buying difficult enough without distortions of the car's history and condition. Kant posited that any mitigation of an individual's autonomy constitutes a violation of the categorical imperative: "Act so that you treat humanity, whether in your own person or in that of another, always as an end and never as a means only" (Martin, 1989, 58).

When lying serves the interests of the liar - and only the liar - it is an act of selfishness. Seligman and Peterson identified universal virtues; it is a reasonable speculation that if they had given themselves to a search for universal vices they would have found lying as one of them. (In spite of its title, Ayn Rand's essay, "The Virtue of Selfishness" does not advocate unbridled self-serving, which would include lying [1961, vii-xii]).

Concluding Thoughts

Lying is akin to speeding in that it is something almost everyone does but admits is wrong. Further, like speeding, it's something most people rationalize but rarely believe anyone else can justify. Lying is recognized as so powerful a temptation that the courts require witnesses to "solemnly swear to tell the truth, the whole truth, and nothing but the truth." (How likely is this thought: "I was fully resolved to lie until I placed my hand on the Bible and promised to tell the truth"?) Regarding "the whole truth," Sissela Bok has written:

> The whole truth is out of reach. But this fact has very little to do with our choices about whether to lie or to speak honestly, about what to say and what to hold back. These choices can be set forth, compared, evaluated, and when they are, even rudimentary distinctions can give guidance (1978, 4).

In his classic, *Man's Search for Meaning*, psychiatrist and Holocaust survivor Viktor Frankl describes his concentration camp resolution to tell the truth and so let his fate be determined.

> In Auschwitz I laid down a rule for myself which proved to to be a good one and which most of my comrades later followed. I generally answered all kinds of questions truthfully. But I was silent

> about anything that was not expressly asked for.
> If I were asked my age, I gave it. If asked about
> my profession, I said "doctor," but did not elabo-
> rate (1959, 74).

How many of us, living in far less dire circumstances, would make the same resolution? (Frankl survived, dying in 1997 at age 93.)

Bok's thorough, scholarly treatise on lying, *Lying: Moral Choice in Private and Public Life*, includes the following chapters (1978):

- Is the "Whole Truth" Attainable?
- Weighing the Consequences
- White Lies
- Lies in a Crisis
- Lying to Liars
- Lying to Enemies
- Lies Protecting Peers and Clients
- Lies for the Public Good
- Deceptive Social Science Research
- Lies to the Sick and Dying

This list implies Bok's agreement with John Stuart Mill's observation: "It is not the fault of any creed, but of the complicated nature of human affairs, that rules of conduct cannot be so framed as to require no exceptions" (Martin, 1989, 64).

In 1920 anthropologist Frederick Starr and attorney Clarence Darrow debated the question, "Is life worth living?" Darrow's introductory statement included this assessment:

> ... man does not live by rules. If he did, he would
> not live. He lives by his emotions, his instincts, his
> feelings; he lives as he goes along. Man does not
> make rules of life and then live according to those
> rules; he lives and then he makes rules of life"
> (MacLaskey and MacLaskey, 1920, 15).

Applying Darrow's thought to lying, children begin life with a rule. They are taught to tell the truth - *always*. Eventually, the complexities of life press upon them; they encounter situations in which their emotions, instincts, and feelings incline them to lie. The rule is amended to accommodate for at least some of those situations. Truth-telling remains the standard and lying is relegated to the category of *the exception to the rule*. Hopefully, with reluctance and regret, it is concluded that life cannot be managed without at least an occasional lie (Malikow, 2011).

20. THE PILLOW ANGEL DEBATE

Medicine is, I have found, a strange and in many ways disturbing business. The stakes are high, the liberties taken tremendous. ... The thing that still startles me is how fundamentally human an endeavor it is.

- Atul Gawande, M.D.

The January 22, 2009 issue of Time *magazine included the story of a controversial medical procedure by which a severely brain-damaged 6 year-old girl's growth had been minimized. The intention of her parents was to enable them to provide better long-term care for her as well as eliminate some complications that would come with her maturation.*

Ashley, now age 9, is a severely brain-damaged girl whose parents decided to have her growth plates closed through high doses of estrogen, thereby limiting her eventual height and weight. In addition, Ashley's uterus was removed to prevent discomfort from menstrual cramps and the possibility of pregnancy in the event of rape. And, because of a family history of cancer, her breast buds were removed. Her parents defended the decision to have these procedures because they will "improve our daughter's quality of life," adding their decision was not motivated by an intention to convenience her caregivers" (Gibbs, 2007). In their blog Ashley's parents explained:

> Ashley's smaller and lighter size makes it more
> possible to include her in the typical family life and
> activities that provide her with needed comfort,
> closeness, security, and love: meal time, car trips,
> touch, snuggles, etc. (2007).

Medical ethicists Dr. Daniel Diekema and Dr. Daniel Gunther defend the now-called "Ashley Treatment" for its medical benefits. Her smaller size not only makes her easier to move around, but with more movement comes improvements in circulation, digestion, muscle tone, and fewer skin sores and infections.

Nevertheless, disability-rights advocates are not convinced the benefits justify the treatment. Those who have weighed in on Ashley's case admit to the the difficulty of caring for a disabled child who will grow to adult size as the parents age and their strength and stamina diminish.

> "I know they love their daughter," says Julia Epstein, communications director for the Disability Rights Education and Defense Fund and mother of a disabled child. "But they refer to her as a pillow angel. I know that's meant to be a sweet term, but it's terminally infantilizing" (2007).

Advocates for the disabled also are concerned that the Ashley Treatment represents the top of a slippery slope. If limiting a disabled person's size to facilitate care for the caregiver is acceptable, will amputations follow for brain-damaged children who are unable to walk? A person with fewer or shorter limbs is easier to transport than one who has full-grown arms and legs. This possibility raises the issue of human dignity - the inherent worth of all people and the respect due them as such. Epstein and others argue the loss of dignity that results from a medically induced permanent childhood outweighs whatever benefits it might provide. Further, it is a physician's work to alleviate pain, and Ashley was not suffering. In addition, advocates ask, why consign a child to an irreversible state when effective therapies for her condition might be forthcoming?

Why the Ashley Treatment Is Ethical

The distinguished philosopher William James, who was also trained as a physician, advocated the view that philosophy must be practical and engage questions in terms of concrete results. This is not to say he agreed with the Machiavellian principle: *the end justifies the means.* James understood that some ends are dishonorable and some means are immoral even if they enable a worthy objective. In Ashley's case, the enrichment of her life is a worthy goal. And since she is unaware of the losses that constitute an ideological problem for disability-rights advocates, there is no loss of dignity.

Ashley's parents made a decision they believed to be in the best interest of their daughter. The fact that these procedures will make their life easier is incidental; it was neither the driving force nor the determining factor for their decision. A review of this case makes clear the procedures would not have been done if caregiver convenience had been the parents' motivation. "I think in the end it was the obvious bond and love that exists between Ashley and her parents that convinced (Ashley's doctors) that this was the right thing to do," concluded Dr. Gunther (2007). A collateral benefit to parents does not make an action immoral. Were that the case, it would be morally wrong to send children to boarding schools or arrange for their adoption, both of which make life easier for parents.

The Ashley Treatment is not a violation of the Hippocratic Oath. An excerpt from the modern version of this affirmation relevant to this case reads:

> I will remember that I do not treat a fever chart,
> a cancerous growth, but a sick human being,
> whose illness may affect the person's family and
> economic stability. My responsibility includes
> these related problems, if I am to care adequate-
> ly for the sick (Lasagna, 1964).

Noteworthy in the oath is the physician's pledge to consider a patient's family. Integral to the quality of Ashley's life is her parents' continuing ability to care for her.

Some opponents of the Ashley Treatment have argued that it does nothing to improve her health and is medically unnecessary for her survival. While this is true, it is also true that doctors routinely agree to procedures that are neither life-saving nor health-enhancing. Cosmetic surgeries and nearly all abortions are elective. And while they are done with the patients' consent, the same is not true for children who have growth hormone treatment to increase their height or orthodontic devices to straighten their teeth. (Ironically, there seems to be no objection to medically enabling a child to be taller.)

Concerning human dignity, can procedures on patients who are unaware of them diminish their dignity? Moreover, is it possible for one person to take the dignity of another? Nancy Kelly, Supervisor of Occupational Therapy at Brigham and Women's Hospital in Boston, believes both are possibilities: "I think one's dignity can be diminished by others even if they are unaware of their situation. Individuals always have the right to be treated with skill, affection, and safety" (2011). Her position has merit; by analogy, the thought of someone covertly photographing or tape recording us is an affront to our dignity. Still, in Ashley's case, if she were aware of her circumstances and could speak, would she choose dignity over physical comfort? Most likely, she would opt for comfort.

The aforementioned slippery slope concern is not totally without merit. Euthanasia of extremely sick infants is legal in the Netherlands and part of a dialog among some medical professionals in Britain (the Royal College of Obstetricians and Gynecologists). Still, the Ashley Treatment has established no legal precedent in this country. On a case-by-case basis each hospital's medical ethics board will grant or deny permission for this procedure.

It cannot be argued convincingly that Ashley's parents acted with indifference to her quality of life. The onus is on those who oppose her parents' decision to explain how Ashley's current body is inferior to the one she had. Further, of what inalienable right has she been deprived? It is an enigmatic assertion that she is entitled to retain the option to have children she could conceive only without her consent, deliver without her comprehension, and never know or nurture. This is not a question of the possibility of her pregnancy, which could occur only in the most despicable of circumstances, but a question of what she loses if her pregnancy is an impossibility. Certain is that all of Ashley's losses are in her favor and none at the expense of her dignity.

The utilitarian philosopher John Stuart Mill has written of "the complex nature of human affairs" that often makes it difficult to determine ethical conduct (Martin, 1989, 64). Dr. Diekema admitted to this ambiguity: "I felt we were doing the right thing for this little girl, but that didn't keep me from feeling a bit of unease. And that's as it should be. Humility is important in a case like this" (2007).

Even Dr. Seuss' teaching, "A person's a person, no matter how small," can be used to support or dispute the Ashley Treatment (Geisel, 1954). Disability-rights advocates would argue that Ashley has a right not to be subjected to medical interventions that shorten her limbs without lengthening her life. Ashley's parents, using the same reference, would say, "Ashley is Ashley, no matter how small."

Thirty centuries ago, Solomon, the King of Israel, rendered a decision in a matter involving an infant who could not speak for himself. Without a legal precedent to guide Solomon, he resorted to the principle of love. He wondered how a loving parent would speak and act on behalf of the child before him. The king's decision is universally lauded as a demonstration of wisdom. Even those who oppose the decision of Ashley's parents do not question their love for her. In the absence of an unambiguous moral guideline, in certain situations the principle of love charts the prudent course. (Malikow)

21. WHO IS A HERO?

Be not afraid of greatness: some are born great, some achieve greatness, and some have greatness thrust upon them.

- William Shakespeare

I have seen the moment of my greatness flicker,
And I have seen the eternal Footman hold my coat, and snicker,
And, in short, I was afraid.

- "The Love Song of J. Alfred Prufrock," T.S. Eliot

Heroes are not born, they are cornered. - Anonymous

In *Everyday Morality*, philosophy professor Mike W. Martin describes this terrifying episode.

> In a wilderness area in a city where I live, a woman was hiking with her five-year-old daughter in 1986. A mountain lion attacked the girl and dragged her into some bushes. The mother's frantic screams were heard by Gregory Ysais, a thirty-six-year-old electronics technician who happened to be hiking in the same area. Without any hesitation Ysais ran to the scene to find the cougar gripping the bloody and squirming child by the back of her neck. Ysais grabbed a branch and repeatedly swung it over the cougar's head. The full-grown cougar responded with threatening roars and quick strikes with his huge paws. After a few minutes the cougar dropped the child long enough for her to be pulled away.

Ysais later reported that he had never been in a life-and-death situation before and had never thought of himself as a hero: "I didn't give it much thought. I just heard people crying for help, and I just ran as fast as I could. I was just doing what I had to do. I couldn't think of anything else" (1986, 121).

Prior to his courageous intervention, Gregory Ysais never thought of himself as a hero. Perhaps he did afterward. Certain is that most people would view his action as heroic even if he did not recognize the danger to himself, calculate the risk, and consider the option of avoidance.

An answer to the question, *Who is a hero?* requires that several other questions first be addressed: *How is hero defined? What are the characteristics that distinguish a hero from a non-hero? Does a single heroic act make a person a hero? Are people heroes if they acted in the line of duty or in response to a calling? Does heroism require the elements of choice and/or overcoming fear? Is it possible to be heroic living an ordinary, unrecognized life?*

How is hero defined?

The *American Heritage Dictionary,* (pp. 617-618) offers six definitions of hero. Two of these definitions will *not* be a part of this treatise: (1) "a sandwich of heroic size made with a small loaf of crusty bread split lengthwise, containing lettuce, condiments, and a variety of meats and cheeses" and, (2) "any male regarded as a potential lover or protector." (My apologies to Subway and Olive Oyl's Popeye.) The four definitions that remain are relevant to the matter at hand; they refer to mythology, courage, fiction, and accomplishment.

In mythology and legend a hero is a being, often born of one mortal and one divine parent, who is favored by the gods, endowed with great courage and strength, and celebrated for bold exploits. Achilles embodies this definition. In *The Iliad*, he ponders the glory that will be his if he remains in Troy and fights in the Trojan War. This glory, however, will be at the expense of his life. (The Greek word for "glory" is *kleos*, the fame which is often heard through a song or poem.)

> My mother Thetis tells me there are two ways in
> which I may meet my end. If I stay here and fight
> then I shall lose my safe homecoming but I will
> have glory that is unwilting. Whereas if I go home
> my glory will die, but it will be a long time be-
> fore the outcome of death shall take me (Homer,
> 1998, 9.410-416).

Perhaps the most common understanding of a hero is one who is noted for feats of courage or nobility of purpose; especially someone who has risked or sacrificed his life. The aforementioned Gregory Ysais fits this description as does the unnamed pilot in Kay Jamison's memoir, *An Unquiet Mind*. Faced with the dilemma of parachuting from his malfunctioning jet to safety or staying with the plane and guiding it away from a schoolyard full of children, he chose the latter and died in a fiery crash. Years later, Jamison, one of those children, wrote of him: "The dead pilot became a hero, transformed into a scorchingly vivid, completely impossible ideal for what was meant by the concept of duty" (1995, 13).

A familiar use of the word hero is "the principle character in a novel, poem, or dramatic presentation" (*American Heritage Dictionary*, 617). *Les Miserables'* Jean Valjean is one of countless literary and theatrical protagonists who fits this characterization (Hugo, 1987).

Individuals of noteworthy achievement often are referred to as heroes. Baseball legend Babe Ruth, Civil War general Robert E. Lee, and civil rights activist Martin Luther King, Jr. are men of accomplishment who enjoy heroic status.

What are the characteristics of a hero?

How is a hero distinguished from a non-hero? In situations that call for heroic action, are there only two possibilities for those in a position to respond? Returning to Gregory Ysais, was he in a situation in which he was going to be either a hero or coward? He acted heroically, but would he have been a coward had he not intervened? Were there only two options available to him: either engage in a struggle with the mountain lion or allow the animal to have its way with the child without interference? Had he stood by and watched, the outcome for the girl would have been the same as if he had walked away from the horrific scene. Further, if he had not intervened, would he be a villain, even though he was not the one bringing harm to the child?

In addition, since Ysais was not seeking an opportunity to act heroically, it is accurate to say that he had greatness thrust upon him. He came upon a crisis and reacted in an exemplary manner. (Interesting is that the Mandarin Chinese characters that combine to be translated *crisis* in English are "danger" and "opportunity.") Certainly, anyone who orchestrated a situation for the purpose of acquiring heroic status would not be a hero. An episode of a television program of many years ago, "Hill Street Blues," featured a police officer who had accidentally shot and killed a little boy. Guilt-ridden and disgraced, he seemed to have made a start at restoring his soiled reputation when he rescued a child from a house fire. When it was discovered that he had arranged for the fire to create an opportunity for heroism his ignominy became even greater.

Does a single act of heroism make a person a hero?

One of the ways in which we can know ourselves is to consider that *we are who we are most of the time* (Malikow, 2010, 106-108). Heroism is but one of 17,953 personality traits (Allport, 1936). Heroism differs from traits that can be demonstrated daily like patience, self-discipline, and generosity. Occasions to act heroically are few, and many people never encounter even one opportunity for a flickering moment of greatness, let alone fifteen minutes of fame.

One way to consider the sufficiency of a single courageous act to establish someone as a hero is to decide if an opportunity generates heroism or elicits it. In *The Wizard of Oz* the Cowardly Lion entering the witch's castle to rescue Dorothy did not create courage in the faltering lion (Baum, 2000). Rather, Dorothy's abduction provided the opportunity for the lion's dormant courage to be activated. The lyrics from the song "Tin Man" include an analysis that also applies to the lion: "Oz never did nothing to the tin man, that he didn't already have" (Bunnell, 2000). This assessment suggests there are people who never encounter a situation that would awaken their latent courage, implying there are many unrealized heroes among us.

This is not to say that courage cannot be developed. What is courage if not the subordination of fear to duty and accomplishing the more difficult thing? Courage requires self-discipline, a trait that can be nurtured. The noted biologist Thomas Huxley was so convinced of this he wrote: "The chief purpose of education is to train a person to do what he ought to do, when it ought to be done, whether he feels like it or not" (Wheelock, 1910, 33). If the potential for heroism resides in any of us, it is because of internalized values that enable us to recognize those things that have greater worth than our comfort, safety and, in rare circumstances, self-preservation. Courage is well described in the movie, "The Princess Diaries:"

> Courage is not the absence of fear but rather the judgment that something else is more important than fear. The brave may not live forever but the cautious do not live at all. From now on you are traveling the road between who you think you are and who you can be. (Cabot, 2008).

Heroes are those whose well-developed self-discipline and discernment enable them to rise to the occasions that call for courage. Courage is not created by those occasions, rather, it is a by-product of the self-discipline, values, and moral code that have developed over time.

"Assume the virtue, if you have it not," wrote Shakespeare (*Hamlet*, 3.4.151). There are virtues that can be feigned, but courage is not one of them. Brave and noble deeds are empirical demonstrations of courage; without courage there would be no courageous acts. For this reason, a single, heroic act is sufficient to qualify an individual as a hero.

However, it is reasonable to ask if subsequent failures of courage call for an individual's reclassification as a coward. An inspirational song asks for, "one moment in time when I'm more than I thought I could be" (Hammond and Bettis, 1988). As previously stated, *we are who we are most of the time*. Notwithstanding, it is also true that *we are who we are in our best moments*. These characterizations are not contradictory. No single maxim can capture the essence of any human being, many are needed. Each one provides a perspective. If only once we have exceeded our self-perceived capability, we have been that person, even if for just one moment in time. A new standard of excellence has been established and with it higher expectations, as well as an increased probability for disappointment.

> *Are people heroes if they acted in the line of duty or*
> *in response to a calling?*

On January 15, 2009 U.S. Airways pilot Chesney "Sully" Sullenberger landed airliner flight 1549 on the Hudson River after a flock of birds collided with the plane, disabling both engines. One-hundred and fifty-five passengers were grateful for this unconventional landing. It would seem odd to question Captain Sullenberger's status as a national hero on the ground that safely landing airplanes is part of his job description. Similarly, it would seem odd, actually ludicrous, to question if firefighters who entered the World Trade Center towers on September 11, 2001 are heroes since entering burning buildings is what they were supposed to do.

"People keep telling me it was a heroic thing to do. In my opinion it was just the right thing to do" (Hartsock, 05/10/10). These are the words of Dave Hartsock, a skydiving instructor who was strapped to his student, Shirley Dygert, in what is called a tandem jump. (Tandem jumps are used in a first jump experience.) When their first parachute opened partially and the reserve chute became entangled in the first one, instructor and student went into a death spiral at 10,000 feet. At 500 feet and descending at 40 miles per hour, Hartsock skillfully managed the control toggles and rotated his position under Dygert so that his body would act as a cushion and break her fall. He is now a quadriplegic with only slight movement in his right arm. Hartsock does not think of himself as a hero. "I was the one who was completely responsible for her safety. What other choices were there?" (Hartsock).

In 1956 Christian missionary Jim Eliot and four of his fellow evangelists were slain by Waudani tribesman in Ecuador. The five men were speared to death by the very people to whom they believe they had been called to present the gospel of Jesus Christ. By virtue of their ultimate sacrifice, these missionaries are martyrs, heroes of the Christian faith. Nobel laureate and humanitarian Mother Teresa of Calcutta also carried on her work in response to a calling, thereby sacrificing whatever other life she might have had. Sainthood, which is her inevitable status, is another expression of religious heroism. These missionaries and Mother Teresa did their work neither as a job nor a profession, but in obedience to a calling. However admirable such obedience might be, can it be considered heroic if it is in response to a divine directive?

Merely doing one's job or carrying out a divinely inspired mission is heroic when the accomplishment is extraordinary or the sacrifice is great. Captain Sullenberger was trained and hired to land airplanes on runways - not rivers. The firefighters who entered the towers of the World Trade Center were trained for extinguishing fires and making rescues in a variety of situations, but not the one that confronted them on 9/11. (As far as we know, none of them refused to go into the towers saying, "Since I am not trained for this, this is not part of my job.")

Does heroism require the elements of choice and/or overcoming fear?

Aristotle's *Principle of the Golden Mean* characterizes a virtue as the apex between two extremes, both of which are vices. From this construction, the virtue of courage is the zenith between the vices of recklessness and cowardice. Recklessness is expressed by action without an appreciation for danger. Without the recognition of danger, there can be no experience of fear. Inaction resulting from the awareness of danger is cowardice. The Aristotilian concept of courage requires action despite fear. The application of the Principle of the Golden Mean to courage gives rise to two questions: *Is an action heroic if it did not require overcoming fear? And, is an action heroic if there was no choice but to act?* Gregory Ysais said he intervened without thinking, making his action more a reflex than a behavior. If he acted without considering the danger and the option of non-involvement, then his reaction does not conform to Aristotle's formula for courage. Similarly, it could be argued that Islamic *jihadist* suicide bombers and World War II Japanese kami-kaze pilots cannot be heroes since their cultural conditioning precluded authentic choice-making.

Further, it is not always clear as to whether or not someone actually has a choice. In 2003 a mountain climber, Aron Ralston, amputated his arm rather than die in a cave, where his arm was hopelessly pinned between the cave's wall and an 800 pound boulder. On the fifth day of his captivity, without a realistic hope of being found, his options were to remain trapped until he died an agonizing death from starvation or experience the excruciating pain of removing his arm with a small knife. Did he really have a choice? (Is it any wonder that the title of his memoir is *Between a Rock and a Hard Place*?)

Individuals who subordinated fear or endured pain to achieve something perceived of greater value have acted commendably, if not heroically. This being said, people also can act heroically without confronting fear or the possibility of avoidance. Reconsider Ysais and Ralston and ask, "Could I have done that?" If your answer is, "I don't think so," or "I don't know, but I would hope so," or "No, but I admire what they did," then this is sufficient to establish them as heroic. Of course, this is a sentimentalist argument. (*Sentimentalism* is the belief that some knowledge cannot be acquired from reason or scientific demonstration, but only from the feeling that something is true.) The counter to this would be a logical argument, perhaps in the form of a syllogism:

Major Premise
All heroic acts include the
subordination of fear and/or
option of avoidance.

Minor Premise
Ysais fighting off a mountain lion
included neither subordination of
fear nor the option of avoidance.

Conclusion
Therefore, Ysais did not engage in a
an act of heroism.

The flaw in this syllogism resides in the major premise. While it may be true that all subordination of fear is a demonstration of heroism, it does not follow that all acts of heroism include the subordination of fear. (The same can be said about the option of avoidance.)

Stanford University psychologist Phil Zombardo, founder of the Heroic Imagination Project, believes that just as a sociopath is the product of nurturing, so also a hero can be developed:

> We have been saddled too long with (a) mystical view of heroism. We assume heroes are demigods. But they're not. A hero is just an ordinary person who does something extraordinary. I believe we can use science to teach people how to do that (Lehrer, 2010).

Is it possible to be a hero living an ordinary, unrecognized life?

It is not customary to buttress a philosophical position by citing a professional athlete. However, an observation made by basketball superstar Charles Barkley is relevant to the question of whether an ordinary, unpublicized person can be a hero. In the wake of the revelation of National Football League quarterback Michael Vick's dog-fighting fiasco, Barkley challenged the assumption that athletes are role models: "Just because I dunk a basketball doesn't mean I should raise your kids" (12/25/10). He vehemently denies that he, Michael Vick, Michael Jordan or any other sports celebrity is a hero or role model for children. Barkley posits that each father bears that responsibility for his own children. Zimbardo agrees with Barkley: "One of the problems with our culture is that we've replaced heroes with celebrities. We worship people who haven't done anything" (Lehrer, 2010). Philosopher Peter Kreeft has made a similar observation: "We honor heroes. We used to have heroes, now we have only sports heroes. They don't even teach the lives of the saints in religion classes anymore" (2007, 68).

For some, a philosophical position articulated by Charles Barkley does not carry sufficient weight to be convincing. (Anyone who has seen Barkley would recognize him as a man who carries considerable weight.)

Such an objection, however, would be an *ad hominem* argument. Heroism is expressed moment-by-moment all over the world when extraordinary, unpublicized acts of virtue occur. This opinion does not devalue heroism, rather it elevates it to something each of us can do, perhaps even frequently. (Malikow)

IV. VALUE THEORY

22. Introductory Thought: What's It Worth to You?

A horse, a horse, my kingdom for a horse.
                                        - King Richard, Act 4, Scene 4

Judge your success by what you had to give up in order to get it.
                                        - The Dalai Lama

What good is it for a man to gain the whole world, yet forfeit his soul.
                                        - Jesus Christ (Mark 8:36)

Value theory is the subcategory of philosophy that addresses the relative worth of things. It pursues answers to questions like, "How do people decide what to take with them when they have to leave their homes because of fire or flood?" and "Why is it cost-effective for the New York Yankees to pay Alex Rodriguez twenty-five million dollars a year?" The worth of something is always assessed in a context. Under normal conditions; air, water, and a match are of no great value. But to a drowning man; a man on fire; and a man freezing in the wilderness; air, water, and a match, respectively, are priceless. A familiar hyperbolic statement is, "I would give my right arm for *x*." Aron Ralston, referred to in the previous chapter, never considered sacrificing his arm until he had to choose between it and his life. Other familiar declarations that imply value judgments are, "I wouldn't trade *x* for anything," and, "Your money or your life?"

In 1972 an airplane carrying a Uruguayan rugby team crashed in the Andes between Argentina and Chile. Several of the survivors resorted to cannibalism, eating flesh from the bodies of those killed in the crash. Like Aron Ralston, they did the unthinkable in order to survive.

It is one thing to believe that no one's life is more valuable than someone else's. Yet, there have been extraordinary situations in which the lives of human beings have been prioritized. The classic example of this is the *dilemma of the lifeboat*, in which decisions had to be made about who would remain in the boat and who would be set adrift, lest the overcrowded vessel sink. In this circumstance, a strong, uninjured man able to row had more value than an elderly, severely wounded survivor.

Given the rarity of self-amputations, decisions about cannibalism, and lifeboat dilemmas, it is understandable to ask: *What is the place of value theory in ordinary life?* Actually, decisions of relative worth are so common they often go unrecognized as instances of value theory. Consider the following examples and do not be surprised if several of them resemble decisions you have made. These examples call for decisions that are neither *right* nor *wrong*. They require a decision based on the establishment of a priority rather than conforming to a principle.

1. You have promised yourself not to withdraw money from your savings account, but the laptop computer you have wanted is on sale. Which is more important to you: a continually growing savings account or the computer?

2. You recently recounted to a friend the joys and benefits of being single. Soon afterward you meet someone and find yourself considering marriage. Which do you value more: freedom without commitment or lifetime companionship with someone you love?

3. You are stopped by a police officer at midnight on a Saturday. When you are asked, "How many drinks have you had?" you are afraid to tell the truth because you have had three glasses of wine in the previous two hours. Although the thought of lying is repugnant to you, you do not believe that you are driving impaired and you are afraid

that the truth will not serve you well. Which do you value more: truthfulness or expediency?

4. The boyfriend (or girlfriend) of one of your friends contacts you to arrange a meeting. When you ask for the reason for the meeting, he (or she) admits to being attracted to you and insists that the meeting be kept a secret. A complicating factor is the attraction you have for your friend's partner. Is this meeting going to take place? Which do you value more, loyalty to a friend or a romantic possibility?

5. You have the opportunity to move into a one-bedroom apartment with a monthly rent of $600. The thought of living alone appeals to you. A friend is also looking for a place to live and asks you if you would like to share a two-bedroom apartment for one-half of the rent. This would cost you $400 per month. The apartments are comparable. It is your preference to live alone, but the opportunity to save $200 per month is attractive. Which do you value more: privacy or saving money?

6. After promising your best friend confidentiality, he confesses that he is sexually attracted to children, although he has never acted on this preference. Since he is an elementary school teacher, you urge him to resign his position. He refuses, claiming that he would never risk his career by being sexually involved with a child. You consider informing the principal of the school where your friend teaches what you know. Which is more important to you: your friend's career and his friendship or the precaution against a child being harmed and your friend going to prison?

Every day we weigh and consider the value of one thing against another. The deliberation can be as mundane as going out for lunch with friends or eating the sandwich made from last night's leftovers, thereby saving money but missing out on an enjoyable time. Or it can be as consequential as leaving a lifeless marriage for a more exciting relationship and the guilt that would accompany that decision. It has been said that decision-making is easy when you know what your values are. Perhaps this is true since the difficulty resides in knowing our values (Malikow, 2009).

23. AIMEE MULLINS THOUGHT EXPERIMENT

Confidence is the sexiest thing a woman can have. It's much sexier than any body part.

- Aimee Mullins

Herman Hesse has written of the road that leads a man to himself. For the man in this story an unplanned encounter in a tavern seems to have paved such a road. As you read, be mindful that there is no "ought" in value theory; "ought" is associated with ethics. Value theory is concerned with understanding why people prefer one thing over another.

Imagine a man sitting at a bar, taking his last sip of Chardonnay before leaving when a stunning woman takes the seat next to him. Without staring, he sizes her up as late-twenties, impeccably dressed with shoulder-length, perfectly coiffed blond hair, a flawless complexion more like porcelain than skin, and mesmerizing blue eyes. Knowing he'll regret not even trying, he begins a conversation and is delighted by her friendliness. More than that, as if more was necessary to rivet his attention, he finds her pleasantly articulate. Over the next hour, from a series of questions designed to keep the conversation going, he learns that she's a Georgetown University graduate where she competed in track-and-field and currently working as an actress and model when not involved in several not-for-profit organizations.

She glances at her watch (fortunately for the first time) and says, "I have an early flight to catch in the morning, I better be going." In synchrony, they rise, extend right hands, and say "Nice to meet you." Emboldened by this serendipitous choreography, he asks for her phone number. As though she expected the question - of course she did, she gets it all the time - she gives him her card, instructing him to use the cell number when he calls.

She leaves without looking back but his eyes never leave her. Returning home with an excitement that precludes falling asleep, he fires up his PC, ostensibly to check for e-mails. Almost immediately he switches to *Google* and mindlessly types in, "Aimee Mullins." In less than a second, the first wave of over 500,000 results appears. After ten minutes of reading he has learned much: She attended Georgetown on a full academic scholarship, one of three awarded by the Department of Defense, graduating with honors from the School of Foreign Service. At seventeen, Aimee was the youngest person ever to hold top-security clearance at the Pentagon, where she worked summers as an intelligence analyst. In 1999 she made her debut as a runway model in London at the invitation of Alexander McQueen, an internationally renown fashion designer. She's appeared in *Vogue*, *Harper's Bazaar*, and *Elle*. In addition, she was in *Esquire's* "Women We Love" issue, *People Magazine* as one of the "50 Most Beautiful People," and on *Rolling Stone's* "Annual Hot List." Aimee also had the starring role in a highly acclaimed film, "Cremaster 3."

She mentioned she's an athlete - that was an understatement. She's featured in exhibits in the NCAA Hall of Fame and Track and Field Hall of Fame and acclaimed in *Sports Illustrated* as one of the "Coolest Women in Sport." At this point he's hardly surprised when reading that the Women's Museum in Dallas, Texas honored her as one of the "Greatest Women of the 20th Century" for her achievements in sports.

The surprise came when he learned that Aimee Mullins is a double amputee! Born without shinbones, both her legs were amputated below the knee when she was a year-old. Her parents decided life with prosthetics would provide her with more mobility than life in a wheelchair. She was born with *fibular hemimelia*, a congenital condition in which large bones in the extremities are absent - a condition that usually occurs in one limb and more often among boys.

More accurately, his reaction was one of shock, not surprise. He had never heard of this condition and there was nothing in Aimee's gait that suggested even an ankle sprain let alone prosthetic legs under her Cynthia Vincent full-length skirt. A cascade of questions followed: Am

I still going to call her? If not, why? Why should "no legs" make a difference? Doesn't this make her all the more impressive? If I do call, how do I bring up what I've learned? ("Oh, I looked you up in *Wikipedia* and learned you're from Allentown, Pennsylvania and that you don't have legs - I mean, real ones.") If I don't call, she'll know why. How can I hurt her by not calling?

He then realized that this is about him, not her. He wondered, "Is it that I don't want to hurt her or that I don't want to generate evidence of my shallowness? And if I do call, would it be to reassure myself that I'm not superficial? After all, she gave me her number, I'm the one wrestling with how to proceed."

More self-examination followed: "Why do I need to date a perfect woman? Isn't that what I thought Aimee was until I learned about her disability? How can I even think of her as disabled? Would she be more accomplished if she had legs? And, what if she had legs but was vain and narcissistic with nothing in her biography but a long history of suitors? Would that make her more desirable?"

Postscript

The preceding thought experiment raises several questions concerning the relative value of human characteristics. What are the qualities that make a person worthy of admiration and acclaim? Does Aimee have these qualities? Should her so-called disability discourage a prospective suitor? If so, why? The sardonic adage "Heroes are not born, they are cornered," implies that acts of extraordinary courage result from situations in which there is no choice but to act heroically. Aimee Mullins did not choose to be born with *fibular hemimelia*, neither did she make the decision for a double amputation. However, throughout her life, she has repeatedly chosen to pursue her interests and test her limits. Is she courageous? Another adage teaches that "Determinism is the hand we've been dealt, free will is the choice of how that hand is played." Aimee Mullins has chosen to "play her hand" by living life to the fullest, challenging and inspiring others to do the same. Is she heroic?

Her resiliency is reminiscent of Dax Cowart, who in 1973 was severely burned in an automobile explosion. In the accident he lost two-thirds of his skin, both hands, both eyes, and both ears. He attempted suicide several times and his appeals to have medical treatment discontinued were denied. Eventually, he accepted his lot as "The Man Sentenced to Life," graduated from law school, and married (Wicker, 1989). Like Aimee Mullins, his recovery from misfortune is remarkable.

Aimee has said, "The only true disability is a crushed spirit" (Lafave, 2010). Certainly she has displayed determination in addition to a host of other favorable qualities: confidence, compassion, intelligence, resilience, and self-discipline. She also has a sense of humor: "Interesting, from an identity standpoint, what does it mean to have a disability? Pamela Anderson has more prosthetics in her body than I do and nobody calls her disabled" (2009). In this age of cosmetic procedures, it is reasonable to ask why artificial legs would be considered unattractive. No doubt, for some men Aimee's admirable traits would not offset what she's lacking below the knee. For others, her prosthetics would be a non-issue. Apparently the author Salman Rushdie is in the latter category; the sixty year-old author and Aimee have been in a relationship for several years.

The thought experiment that constitutes the first part of this essay provides an opportunity to consider some of the 17,953 traits that contribute to personality (Allport, 1936). Moreover, it provides an occasion for reflection upon our own values - those we admire in others and seek for ourselves. (Malikow)

24. A TIME TO KILL

There is a time for everything, and a season for every activity under heaven. ... a time to kill and a time to heal.

- Ecclesiastes 3:1,3

And God spoke all these words: ... You shall not murder.

- Exodus 20: 1,13

In 1984 at the De Soto County courthouse in Hernando, Mississippi, John Gresham, then a 29 year-old attorney, heard the testimony of a 12 year-old girl in which she described her brutal rape and beating at the hands of two men. Although not involved in the case, Gresham wondered what would happen if the girl's father murdered her daughter's assailants. Would a jury - *could a jury* - find a man guilty if he avenged the rape and near-death beating of his little girl by killing the men responsible?

The result of Gresham's rumination is the novel, *A Time to Kill*, a book that took him three years to write since he worked a few hours at a time, starting at 5 a.m. before attending to his practice (1989). After several publishers had rejected it, *A Time to Kill* had a modest first printing (5,000 copies) in 1988. In 1996 it was adapted to film with a cast that includes, Sandra Bullock, Samuel L. Jackson, Ashley Judd, Matthew McConaughey, Kevin Spacey, and Donald and Kiefer Sutherland.

The philosophical issues that arise from this case are several and certainly include the father's weighing of vengeance against his imprisonment. The former would provide justice (in the father's sight); the latter would deprive his family of a provider, husband, and father. Weighing and considering one possibility against another constitute an exercise in *value theory*.

Dramatic presentations as books or movies exceed the ability of brief descriptions to generate pathos. Rather than using this summary to consider the relative value of satisfaction derived from vengeance to the ramifications of incarceration, a reading of *A Time to Kill* or viewing of its film version will evoke the requisite emotions for meaningful thought and discussion. (Malikow)

25. CAN A LIFE BE WASTED?

A clean house is a sign of a wasted life.

- Anonymous

The issue of a "wasted life" is directly addressed in the popular 1997 movie "Good Will Hunting." The protagonist, Will Hunting, is a genius beyond measure with unlimited intellectual interests. Yet, he chooses to work construction and hang out with his less cerebral friends in South Boston. Eventually, Will's best friend challenges him to stop wasting his life, positing that Will's extraordinary intellect requires him to do something more than swing a sledge hammer by day and drink beer by night.

Is it possible for a life to be wasted? Is Will Hunting living a wasted life because he's not utilizing his exceptional intelligence by working as a laborer? If so, does it follow that 6'9" tall bestselling author Michael Crichton should have played basketball instead of writing? Is a person with an extraordinary attribute or capability obligated to use that characteristic, talent or skill? If so, from where does this obligation originate? Phrases such as "God-given ability" and "gift from God" are hardly compelling for an atheist or agnostic.

Can a life be wasted? This question can be understood as an ethical issue because it implies there are *right* and *wrong* ways for spending a life. Perhaps Crichton should be excused for not playing basketball since he pursued a career as a writer and was hugely successful. (His book sales have exceeded 150,000,000 copies.) Crichton also graduated from Harvard Medical School without ever practicing medicine. Was he supposed to be a physician? Was his decision to be a writer in any sense closer to *right* than Will Hunting's?

The question of a wasted life also can be understood as a value theory issue since it involves comparing the worth of possible lives. Waste occurs when something it is used for its other than intended purpose. In addition, something can be considered wasted when it is used to serve an inferior purpose or, even worse, a meaningless cause. In a drought, people are urged not to waste water by washing cars or watering lawns. When a family's breadwinner is unemployed, money is in short supply and not to be wasted on luxuries. Framed in this manner, a problem arises when presuming to speak of a life as wasted. Who determines how anyone's life ought to be used? On what basis can one person declare to another that she is wasting her life?

Curious is that each of us enters this world through no choice of our own, yet are told that we are responsible for doing something meaningful with our lives. (*Antinatalists* are among the philosophers who disagree that any such responsibility exists. They believe it would be better to have never been born. Professor David Benatar has written extensively on this subject in his book, *Better Never to Have Been [2006]*).

An essay that appeared in *Newsweek* magazine the week of Mother's Day, 2010, also addresses the issue of the worthy use of a life. The author, Julia Baird, challenged the widely held view that good mothers sacrifice their careers to devote themselves to their children. Not only does she believe that being a good mother does not require choosing maternity over the pursuit of other interests, but also believes there's nothing wrong with subordinating motherhood to those interests.

Baird wrote favorably of Nobel laureate Doris Lessing who left two toddlers behind to pursue her work as a writer. Concerning this decision, Lessing said:

> For a long time I thought I had done a very brave thing. There is nothing more boring for an intelligent woman than to spend endless amounts of time with small children. I felt I wasn't the best person to bring them up. I would have ended up an alcoholic or a frustrated intellectual like my mother (Baird, 2010).

Baird does not explicitly defend Lessing's choice to renege on motherhood. However, she does encourage women to combine career and family without feeling guilty, falsely believing that they must be giving their children short shrift.

> Today women no longer need to escape their families to work or be happy - now they need to escape their own unrealistic expectations of what a good mother is. ... that impossible ideal of the perfect mother has become a tyranny.
>
> ... Now that we are allowed to be more than mothers, we wonder if we have the time to be anything but mothers if we are to be truly good" (2010).

Eric Hoffer, one of America's best known philosophers, had a unique life that nearly ended by suicide at age 29. Not particularly depressed, he took stock of his life in 1931 and decided not to continue the "deadening routine of a workingman's life in the city" (Hoffer, 1983, 25). A flash of insight aborted his suicide, which was already in progress. He went on to write ten books and numerous articles on social philosophy while working as a longshoreman. If Hoffer had accomplished his suicide, would he have wasted his life? If he had worked as a longshoreman without writing anything, would that have been a wasted life?

The thought that one person would presume to assess another person's life as wasted is repugnant to existentialists. For them, there is no ideal against which to evaluate anyone's life - we create ourselves through our actions, not by conforming to a standard others have set for us. Jean-Paul Sartre, Albert Camus, and Friedrich Nietzsche all wrote that we bear responsibility for our own life without any tinge of obligation to live as others think we ought. The existential view of Hoffer's life is that he lived as he chose to live; his life simply was. It would have been no better or worse had he opted to live differently. The concept of a wasted life is meaningful only to those who believe certain conditions require a life to be spent prescriptively. Apart from an authoritative prescription, a life cannot be wasted. (Malikow)

26. MOTHER TERESA'S BUREAUCRATIC ENCOUNTER

Attorney Philip K. Howard's 1996 bestseller, The Death of Common Sense, *includes instances of the law being valued over reason and pragmatism. One of his illustrations is Mother Teresa's thwarted effort to provide a homeless shelter in New York City.*

In the winter of 1988, nuns of the Missionaries of Charity were walking through the snow in the South Bronx in their saris and sandals to look for an abandoned building that they might convert into a homeless shelter. Mother Teresa, the Nobel Prize winner and head of the order, had agreed on the plan with Mayor Ed Koch after visiting him in the hospital several years earlier. The nuns came to two fire-gutted buildings on 148th Street and, finding a Madonna among the rubble, thought perhaps that providence itself had ordained the mission. New York City offered the abandoned buildings at one dollar each, and the Missionaries of Charity set aside $500,000 for the reconstruction. The nuns developed a plan to provide temporary care for sixty-four homeless men in a communal setting that included a dining room and kitchen on the first floor, a lounge on the second floor, and small dormitory rooms on the third and fourth floors. The only unusual thing about the plan was that Missionaries of Charity, in addition to their vow of poverty, avoid the routine use of modern conveniences. There would be no dishwashers or other appliances; laundry would be done by hand. For New York City the proposed homeless facility would be (literally) a godsend.

Although the city owned the buildings, no official had the authority to transfer them except through an extensive bureaucratic process. For a year and a half the nuns, wanting only to live a life of ascetic service, found themselves instead traveling in their sandals from hearing room to hearing room, presenting the details of the project and then discussing the details at two higher levels of city government. In September 1989 the city finally approved the plan and the Missionaries of Charity began repairing the fire damage.

Providence, however, was no match for law. New York's building code, they were told after almost two years, requires an elevator in every new or renovated multiple-story building.

The Missionaries explained that because of their beliefs they would never use the elevator, which would also add upward of $100,000 to the project. The nuns were told that the law could not be waived even if an elevator didn't make sense.

Mother Teresa gave up. She didn't want to devote that much extra money to something that really wouldn't help the poor: according to her representative, "The Sisters felt they could use the money much more usefully for soup and sandwiches." In a polite letter to the city expressing their regrets, the Missionaries of Charity noted that the episode "served to educate us about the law and its many complexities" (Howard, 1996, 3-4).

27. Solvay Teacher Admits He Had Sex Relationship with Pupil, 16

The value of some things can be measured monetarily - but not everything can be appraised in this way. In the following news story, a young high school teacher valued his relationship with one of his students enough to risk his career to pursue her. Time will tell if his assessment was misguided.

A Solvay High School teacher is losing his job and will be required to register as a sex offender after admitting in court Thursday to having an improper sexual relationship with a 16 year-old student.

Kolbee Kearns, 24, of 178 Sunhill Terrace, pleaded guilty before Onondaga County Judge Anthony Aloi to a felony charge of third-degree criminal sexual act. He admitted to engaging in an act of oral sexual conduct with a 16 year-old girl at a location in the city of Syracuse in January. As part of the plea deal, Aloi agreed to sentence Kearns to 10 years probation with four months to be served in the county penitentiary in Jamesville. Sentence is set for September 17.

Kearns must also resign from the Solvay school district and sign an agreement to turn in his teaching certificate before sentencing. Kearns had been in his second year as a probationary science teacher. Defense lawyer Thomas Ryan said the plea satisfied additional charges pending or being contemplated. Assistant District Attorney Janice Fall said Kearns was arrested in March after his relationship with the girl came to the attention of school officials and law enforcement authorities. An order of protection was issued directing Kearns to have no contact with the teenager, she said.

But Kearns was arrested again in May on charges he violated that order by seeing the girl again, Fall said. Authorities were also investigating whether he had ben violating the no-contact order by making phone calls, the prosecutor said.

Aloi said the now 17 year old victim gave authorities a statement indicating she and Kearns were in love and planned to remain together. The judge also took note of Kearns youthful appearance. "He looks like a high school student himself. But that's no excuse for this conduct," Aloi said.

Although the judge said there was nothing sinnister about the relationship, he said it resulted in Kearns having a felony conviction being forced to register as a sex offender and losing his profession. The fact that Kearns and the teenager may be in love "does not make this relationship any less appropriate," the judge said.

Aloi allowed Kearns to remain free on bail pending sentencing and told him he must continue to obey the order of protection (O'Hara, 2010).

28. THE BENEFITS OF
RESTLESSNESS AND
JAGGED EDGES

I have often asked myself whether, given the choice, I would choose to have manic-depressive illness. ... Strangely enough I think I would choose to have it. ... I honestly believe that because of it I have felt more things more deeply. ... Depressed, I have crawled on my hands and knees in order to get across a room and have done it for month after month. But, normal or manic, I have run faster, thought faster, and loved faster than most I know.

- Kay Redfield Jamison

Kay Redfield Jamison is a professor of psychiatry at the Johns Hopkins School of Medicine. Her superbly written memoir, An Unquiet Mind, recounts the mental illness that has plagued and energized her - bipolar disorder (1995). In this essay she expresses the value of the intense passion and enthusiasm that characterizes this illness without dismissing its liabilities.

I believe that curiosity, wonder, and passion are defining qualities of imaginative minds and great teachers; that restlessness and discontent are vital things; and intense experience and suffering instruct us in ways less intense emotions can never do. I believe, in short, we are equally beholden to heart and mind, and that those who have particularly passionate temperaments and questioning minds leave the world a different place for their having been there. It is important to value intellect and discipline, of course, but it is also important to recognize the importance of irrationality, enthusiasm, and vast energy. Intensity has its costs, of course - in pain, in hastily and poorly reckoned plans, in impetuousness - but it has its advantages as well.

Like millions of Americans, I was dealt a hand of intense emotions and volatile moods. I have had manic-depressive illness, also known as bipolar disorder, since I was eighteen years old. It is an illness that ensures that those who have it will experience a frightening, chaotic, and emotional ride. It is not a gentle or easy disease. And, yet, from it I have come to see how important a certain restlessness and discontent can be in one's life; how important the jagged edges and pain can be in determining the course and force of one's life.

I have often longed for peace and tranquility - looked into the lives of others and envied a kind of calmness - and yet I don't know if this tranquility is what I truly would have wished for myself. One is, after all, only really acquainted with one's own temperament and way of going through life. It is best to acknowledge this, to accept it, and to admire the diversity of temperaments nature has dealt us.

An intense temperament has convinced me to teach not only from books, but from what I have learned from experience. So I try to impress upon young doctors and graduate students that tumultuous-ness, if coupled to discipline and a cool mind, is not such a bad sort of thing. That unless one wants to live a stunningly boring life, one ought to be on good terms with one's darker side and one's darker energies. And, above all, that one should learn from turmoil and pain, share one's joy with those less joyful, and encourage passion when it seems likely to promote the common good.

Knowledge is marvelous, but wisdom is even better (Jamison, 2005).

29. THE DISPARITY BETWEEN INTELLECT AND CHARACTER

This essay appeared in the September 22, 1995 Chronicle of Higher Education. Written by Harvard professor, psychiatrist, and Pulitzer Prize author Robert Coles, he challenges his colleagues - at all universities - to reflect and act on their responsibility to engage in effective character education.

Over 150 years ago Ralph Waldo Emerson gave a lecture at Harvard University, which he ended with a terse assertion: "Character is higher than intellect." Even then, this prominent man of letters was worried (as many other writers and thinkers of succeeding generations would be) about the limits of knowledge and the nature of a college's mission. The intellect can grow and grow, he knew, in a person who is smug, ungenerous, even cruel. Institutions originally founded to teach their students how to become good and decent, as well as broadly and deeply literate, may abandon the first mission to concentrate on a driven, narrow book learning - a course of study in no way intent on making a connection between ideas and theories on one hand and, on the other, our lives as we actually live them.

Students have their own way of realizing and trying to come to terms with the split that Emerson addressed. A few years ago, a sophomore student of mine came to see me in great anguish. She had arrived at Harvard from a Midwestern, working-class background. She was trying hard to work her way through college, and, in doing so, cleaned the rooms of some of her fellow students. Again and again, she encountered classmates who had apparently forgotten the meaning of *please*, of *thank you* - no matter how high their Scholastic Assessment Test scores - students who did not hesitate to be rude, even crude toward her.

One day she was not so subtly propositioned by a young man she knew to be a very bright, successful pre-med student and already an accomplished journalist. This was not the first time he had made such an overture, but now she had reached a breaking point. She had quit her job and she was preparing to quit college in what she called "fancy, phony Cambridge."

The student had been part of a seminar I teach, which links Raymond Carver's fiction and poetry with Edward Hopper's paintings and drawings - the thematic convergence of literary and artistic sensibility in exploring American loneliness, both its social and personal aspects. As she expressed her anxiety and anger to me, she soon was sobbing hard. After her sobbing quieted, we began to remember the old days of that class. But she had some weightier matters on her mind and began to give me a detailed, sardonic account of college life, as viewed by someone vulnerable and hard-pressed by it. At one point, she observed of the student who had propositioned her: "The guy gets all A's. He tells people he's in Group I (the top academic category). I've taken two moral reasoning courses with him, and I'm sure he's gotten A's in both of them - and look at how he behaves with me, and I'm sure with others."

She stopped for a moment to let me take that in. I happened to know the young man and could only acknowledge the irony of his behavior, even as I wasn't totally surprised by what she'd experienced. But I was at a loss to know what to say to her. A philosophy major, with a strong interest in literature, she had taken a course on the Holocaust and described for me the ironies she also saw in that tragedy - mass murder of unparalleled historical proportion in a nation hitherto known as one of the most civilized in the world, with a citizenry as well educated as that of any country at the time.

Drawing on her education, the student put before me names such as Martin Heidegger, Carl Jung, Paul DeMan, Ezra Pound - brilliant and accomplished men (a philosopher, a psychoanalyst, a literary critic, a poet) who nonetheless linked themselves with the hate that was Naziism and Fascism in the 1930s. She reminded me of the willingness of the leaders of German and Italian universities to embrace Nazi and

Fascist ideas, of the countless doctors and lawyers and judges and jour-nalists and schoolteachers, and, yes, clergy - who were able to acco-modate themselves to murderous thugs because the thugs had political power. She pointedly mentioned, too, the Soviet Gulag, that expanse of prisons to which millions of honorable people were sent by Stalin and his brutish accomplices - prisons commonly staffed by psychiatrists quite eager to label those victims of a vicious totalitarian state with an assortment of psychiatric names, then shoot them up with drugs meant to reduce them to zombies.

I tried hard, at the end of a conversation that lasted almost two hours, to salvage something for her, for myself, and, not least for a uni-versity that I much respect, even as I know its failings. I suggested that if she had learned what she had just shared with me at Harvard - why, *that* was itself a valuable education acquired. She smiled, gave me credit for a "nice try," but remained unconvinced. Then she put this tough, pointed, unnerving question to me: "I've been taking all these philoso-phy courses, and we talk about what's true, what's important, what's *good*. Well, how do you teach people to *be* good?" And, she added: "What's the point of *knowing* good, if you don't keep trying to *become* a good person?"

I suddenly found myself on the defensive, although all along I had been sympathetic to her, to the indignation she had been directing toward some of her fellow students, and to her critical examination of the limits of abstract knowledge. Schools are schools, colleges are colleges, I averred, a complacent and smug accommodation in my voice. Thereby I meant to say that our schools and colleges these days don't take major responsibility for the moral values of their students, but, rather, assume that their students acquire those values at home. I topped off my surrender to the *status quo* with a shrug of my shoulders, to which she responded with an unspoken but barely concealed anger. This she expressed through a knowing look that announced she'd taken the full moral measure of me.

Suddenly, she was on her feet preparing to leave. I realized that I had stumbled badly. I wanted to pursue the discussion, applaud her for taking on such a large subject in a forthright, incisive manner, and tell her she was right in understanding that moral reasoning is not to be equated with moral conduct. I wanted, really, to explain my shrug - point out that there is only so much any of us can do to affect others' behavior, that institutional life has its own momentum. But she had no interest in that kind of self-justification - as she let me know in an unforgettable aside as she was departing my office: "I wonder whether Emerson was just being 'smart' in that lecture he gave here. I wonder if he ever had any ideas about what to *do* about what was worrying him - or did he think he'd done enough because he'd spelled out the problem to those Harvard professors?"

She demonstrated that she understood two levels of irony: One was that the study of philosophy - even moral philosophy or moral reasoning - doesn't necessarily prompt in either the teacher or the student a determination to act in accordance with moral principles. And, further, a discussion of that very irony can prove equally sterile - again carrying no apparent consequences as far as one's everyday actions go.

When that student left my office (she would soon leave Harvard for good), I was exhausted and saddened - and brought up short. All too often those of us who read books or teach don't think to pose for ourselves the kind of ironic dilemma she had posed to me. How might we teachers encourage our students (encourage *ourselves*) to take that big step from thought to action, from moral analysis to fulfilled moral commitments? Rather obviously, community service offers us all a chance to put our money where our mouths are; and, of course, such service can enrich our understanding of the disciplines we study. A reading of *Invisible Man* (literature), *Tally's Corner* (sociology and anthropology), or *Children and Society* (psychology and psychoanalysis) takes on new meaning after some time spent in the ghetto or a clinic. By the same token, such books can prompt us to think pragmatically about, say, how the wisdom of Ralph Ellison worked to his fiction might shape the way we get along with the children we're tutoring - affect our attitudes toward them, the things we say and do with them.

Yet, I wonder whether classroom discussion, *per se*, won't also be of help, the skepticism of my student notwithstanding. She had pushed me hard, and I started referring again and again in my classes on moral introspection to what she had observed and learned, and my students more than got the message. Her moral righteousness, her shrewd eye and ear for hypocrisy hovered over us, made us uneasy, goaded us.

She challenged us to prove that what we think intellectually can be connected to our daily deeds. For some of us, the connection was established through community service. But that is not the only possible way. I asked students to write papers that told of particular efforts to honor through action the high thoughts we were discussing. Thus goaded to a certain self-consciousness, I suppose, students made various efforts. I felt that the best of them were small victories, brief epiphanies that might otherwise have been overlooked, but had great significance for the students in question.

"I thanked someone serving me food in the college cafeteria, and then we got to talking, for the first time," one student wrote. For her, this was a decisive break from her former indifference to others she abstractly regarded as "the people who work on the serving line." She felt that she had learned something about another's life and had tried to show respect for that life.

The student who had challenged me with her angry, melancholy story had pushed me to teach differently. Now, I make an explicit issue of the more than occasional disparity between thinking and doing, and I ask my students to think about how we might all bridge that disparity. To be sure, the task of connecting intellect to character is daunting, as Emerson and others well knew. And any of us can lapse into cynicism, turn the moral challenge of a seminar into yet another moment of opportunism: I'll get an A this time, by writing a paper cannily exposing myself as a doer of this or that "good deed"!

Still, I know that college administrators and faculty members everywhere are struggling with the same issues that I was faced with, and I can testify that many students will respond seriously, in at least small ways, if we make clear that we really believe that the link between moral reasoning and action is important to us. My experience has given me at least a measure of hope that moral reasoning and reflection can somehow be integrated into students' - and teachers' - lives as they actually live them (Coles, 1995).

V. AESTHETICS

30. Introductory Thought: Beauty and the Experience of Pleasure

*Medicine, law, engineering - these are noble pursuits and neces-
sary to sustain life. But love, romance, passion - these are what we
stay alive for.*

> \- Mr. Keating, "Dead Poets Society"

See how she leans her cheek upon her hand!
O, that I were a glove upon that hand.
That I might touch that cheek!

> \- Romeo and Juliet, 2.2

We relate to the world through five senses and every now and then
are enchanted by something we hear - a new song that makes us rush to
the music store; something we smell - a perfume's fragrance; or someone we see - "I saw you from across the room and just have to know
you." Why do we take delight in beauty?

> Aesthetics refers to those things that are pleasing
> to the senses; beautiful to see or hear. The aes-
> thetic questions are: What makes someone or
> something aesthetically pleasing? How is beauty
> determined? What constitutes a work of art or a
> classic? (Malikow, 2009, xi)

Yale University psychology professor Paul Bloom is convinced that an explanation of the experience of pleasure is integral to an understanding of human nature:

> ... if you look through a psychology textbook, you will find little or nothing about sports, art, music, drama, literature, play and religion. These are central to what makes us human, and we won't understand any of them until we understand pleasure (2010, xiv).

While it seems that psychologists have given short shrift to beauty and the experience of pleasure, philosophers have not. Immanuel Kant posited that beauty cannot be associated with usefulness or monetary value. He agreed with Ralph Waldo Emerson's observation: "Beauty is its own excuse for being" (1847). On the other hand, G.E. Moore and David Hume disagreed on the matter of beauty. Specifically, they had different answers to the question: *Is beauty determined by the observer or the thing observed?* In other words, is beauty recognized or assigned? The former would mean beauty is in the object; the latter would mean something is beautiful because certain people or a substantial number of people declare it to be so. (This issue is similar to the well-known philosophical conundrum: If a tree falls in the forest and no one is present to hear it, is there still a noise?) Moore maintained that beauty is in the object, even if no one recognizes it as such. By analogy, a right triangle has the characteristic of a 90 degree angle even if no one sees it. Similarly, the beauty of a sunset is not determined by the number of people who gaze upon it. It is no less beautiful if one person sees it rather than a hundred - or even if no one sees it.

David Hume held a *sentimentalist* view of beauty. He believed the experience of beauty cannot be rationalized, it is merely felt. It is akin to Pascal's characterization of faith, "The heart has its reasons of which reason knows nothing" (1966). An appeal of Hume's conclusion is that it accounts for the disparity of opinions concerning beauty. Even if there is universal agreement about sunsets, the same cannot be said about paintings, music, and the physical attractiveness of human beings. (For example, with regard to physical attractiveness, Miss Americas since 2000 are considerably taller, yet weigh less when compared to their predecessors from 1950 and earlier.)

A mediating position between those of Moore and Hume is that beauty is a confluence of recognition and declaration. For instance, a book achieves bestseller status owing to public acclaim, but the book has qualities that account for its popularity. Acclaim does not converge randomly upon books, paintings, and symphonies. Universal recognition comes from universal appeal and universal appeal emanates from a created work's intrinsic qualities. Vincent Van Gogh's "Sunflowers," which had no buyers in his lifetime but sold at auction for 39.9 million dollars in 1987, never changed.

> Art collectors in Van Gogh's day saw the same images and colors on canvas seen by contemporary art collectors. Yet, the perceptions of the two groups are very different. Whatever the explanation for this difference, it involves both aesthetics and value theory (Malikow, 2009, 24).

Could it be the art community had to mature in order to appreciate "Sunflowers'" inherent beauty?

As previously stated, the five senses mediate the environment to us. A consideration of three of these senses (hearing, tasting, and smelling) is sufficient to demonstrate the complexity of how pleasure works.

It is not necessary to be a trained musician to have an experience that is pleasing to the ear. Rarely, if ever, are people asked *if* they like music. Instead they are asked what *kind of* music they enjoy. While musical preferences vary, there are pieces that have achieved *classic* status because of their widespread appeal over several generations. Handel's "Messiah" is in this category. Concerning musical preferences, neuroscientists Robert Sapolsky and Daniel Levitin independently have concluded that people are approximately 20 years-old or younger when they hear the music they're going to listen to for the rest of their lives.

> We lock in our musical preference when we affiliate with a particular social group - in the late teens or early twenties. As economist Tyler Cowen put it: "The problem with old music is simple. *Somebody else liked it*. Even worse, that somebody might have been our parents" (Bloom, 2010, 128- 129).

Further, while *favorite singers* vary from one person to another, no one has a favorite singer who cannot carry a tune. Even those who do not have Karen Carpenter or Josh Groban as their favorite singer would concede that both have passable voices.

A chocolatier's advertisement asks, "Do you dream in chocolate?" What is it about the taste of chocolate that makes it more alluring than broccoli? Researchers found that chocolate acts on the brain in a manner similar to that of marijuana. Cannabinoid is the active compound in marijuana that inhibits the breakdown of a substance in the brain and accounts for the good feeling marijuana produces. Chocolate also inhibits the breakdown of this brain substance (anandamide) resulting in a euphoric experience (di Tomaso, Beltsano, and Piomelli, 1996). In addition, what people believe about something influences their experience. (This is known as *psychological set*.) It is safe to say that most Americans would not eat a chocolate covered ant and would be repulsed if informed they had been tricked into doing so. The movie "The Prince of Tides" includes a scene in which a man enjoys his dish of fried dogfood, believing his wife has served him a special meal. The reality of psychological set is sufficient to generate wondering if people really can distinguish between a three dollar Starbuck's coffee and the convenience store's one dollar brew.

The adage, "wake up and smell the roses" implies that the olfactory pleasantness of roses provides an incentive to arise. Shakespeare wrote, "a rose by any other name would smell as sweet," conveying the idea that the reality of things is unaffected by what they are called (*Romeo and Juliet*, 2.2). Research, however, supports neither this adage nor Shakespeare's assertion. Psychological set also influences the experience of smell. One study showed that delight or revulsion depended on what the subjects had been told about what they were smelling. They were exposed to the same odor (cheese), but some were told they were smelling cheese and others that it was vomit. The subjects reacted with pleasure or repugnance according to what they had been told (Finger, Silver, and Restrepo, 2000).

The cheese/vomit experiment demonstrates that what we believe about things we smell influences our interpretation of an odor. The same is true for the other senses. Sensing and perceiving are different operations. Sensations are conveyed by the organs that enable seeing, hearing, tasting, feeling, and smelling. Perceptions are interpretations of sensations. An experiment conducted by Professor Bruce Hood shows that perceptions influenced by psychological set can't always be explained.

> One day he brought a sweater to class and asked students if any of them would be willing to wear it for a small amount of money. Every student indicated willingness with a raised hand. When he proceeded to tell the class that the sweater once belonged to a serial murderer, nearly every hand went down. A neuroscientist, Dr. Hood has coined the term *supersense* to describe the beliefs that people hold but cannot explain. He believes that our brains are designed to make sense of our experiences, including things we are told. This penchant often leads to unscientific explanations and irrational beliefs. It seems that sometimes superstition provides the illusion of control in the face of mystery (Malikow, 2010, 23).

What the students believed about the sweater made it more than a mere sweater and influenced their feeling about it as well as their decision not to wear it. This is similar to the experience of many Roman Catholics when participating in the Eucharist (also referred to as Holy

Communion). The ingestion of wine and wafer in this sacrament has an emotional consequence because the elements are received as the body and blood of Jesus Christ, owing to a sacramental miracle. Our associations with the objects of our sensual experiences are as various as our personal histories. This diversity accounts for why a song or movie or aroma that brings a fond memory to one person provokes anxiety or even bitter tears in another. For this reason, many aesthetic experiences have a complexity that makes it impossible to fully explain them. (Malikow)

31. At War with My Skin

Over thirty years ago the New Yorker *published John Updike's essay, "From the Diary of a Leper." In his memoir,* Self-Consciousness, *he devoted an entire chapter to the condition that plagued him from age six to the end of his life in 2009. Dysmorphia is the psychological term for an exaggerated attentiveness to a bodily feature. If not dysmorphia, Updike certainly displays an acute awareness of his perceived unattractiveness.*

Psoriasis keeps you thinking. Strategies of concealment ramify, and self-examination is endless. You are forced to the mirror, again and again; psoriasis compels narcissism, if we can suppose a Narcissus who did not like what he saw. In certain lights, your face looks passable; in slightly different other lights, not. Shaving mirrors and rearview mirrors in automobiles are merciless, whereas the smoky mirrors in airplane bathrooms are especially flattering and soothing: one's face looks as tawny as a movie star's. Flying back from the Caribbean, I used to admire my improved looks; years went by before I noticed that I looked equally good, in the lavatory glow, on the flight down. I cannot pass a reflecting surface on the street without glancing in, in hopes that I have somehow changed. Nature and the self, the great moieties of earthly existence, are each cloven in two by a fascinated ambivalence. One hates one's abnormal, erupting skin but is led into a brooding, solicitous attention toward it. One hates the Nature that has imposed this affliction, but only this Nature can be appealed to for erasure, for cure. Only Nature can forgive psoriasis; the sufferer in his self-contempt does not grant to other people this power. Perhaps the unease of my first memory has to do with my mother's presence; I wished to be alone in the sun, the air, the distant noises, the possibility of my hideousness going away (Updike, 1989).

32. In Love with an Android

In Pragmatism *(1955) William James articulated his view that in order for philosophy to have value it must be practical. He argued that philosophers are doing the work they ought to be doing when they are providing answers to real-life questions and solutions to real-life problems. James seems to be contradicting himself with his theoretical "mechanical sweetheart." However, its practical application is a response to Immanuel Kant's question: What is a human being? The "mechanical sweetheart" raises several questions, including whether or not an android would be an attractive lover and, if not, why? In* Doing Philosophy *Thomas Ellis Katen describes James' thought experiment.*

Suppose you meet the perfect mate, someone ideal in every respect, and who does everything you want. Further, this wonderful mate fulfills the sexual relationship. This mate is physically attractive and, as it is said, very well built. There is one problem, and it is that this mate is really well built because it was constructed rather than born. Your potential spouse is an *android*. Thus you will have a mate who will have everything - everything, that is, but a soul. If you are a woman, would you marry your dream man if you discovered he was missing a soul? If you are a man, would you marry your dream woman if you found out she was minus a soul?

... A fundamental metaphysical issue is at stake here, for if this android did everything a human did and differed only in one respect, that of not having a soul, how would one *know* the difference? Where is the soul? What is it? What difference does it make? Unless someone tells you this is an android, would you ever miss *soul*? If soul makes no behavioral differences, do we have any basis for assuming it exists? And if it does make behavioral differences, just what are they?

... What about man? Must he be understood as a part of nature in physicochemical terms, or is there something distinctive about man? Is he set off from the rest of nature by possessing an immaterial dimension in his being, a soul? (1973, 120)

33. Of Course Priests Fall in Love

Few people wear as many hats successfully as Andrew Greeley: Roman Catholic priest, sociologist, professor, journalist, and novelist. A prolific writer, his bestselling fictional works include The Cardinal Sins, Thy Brother's Wife, *and* Ascent into Hell; *titles not to be expected from a priest. The following essay is typical of Father Greeley's unflinching willingness to address sensitive issues as well as his ability to do so with kindness and clarity.*

At the risk of scandalizing both Catholics and anti-Catholics, I'm going to reveal a secret: Priests have hormones. They also have fantasies. They even fall in love. All of these phenomena cover an even more ugly secret: Priests are male members of the human race - and soon may include female members of the human race who also, be it noted, have hormones, fantasies, and a propensity to fall in love.

In a TV interview about one of my novels, the woman newscaster opined that "for a priest" there was a lot of sex in the novel. There was not all that much sex, to tell the truth, and none of it was graphic or clinical or prurient (which may make it more erotic than less). She then added, "Of course priests don't fall in love."

To her dismay I replied that they sure do and that, to anticipate her next question, I had fallen in love lots of times.

Human beings fall in love - in the sense of being powerfully attracted to someone else. They also fall in love - in the sense of forming deep and lasting affection for someone else. At last count priests were human beings. Why should they be thought to be immune from these delightful, poignant, frustrating, discouraging, disconcerting and fascinating experiences?

Why? Because the church for a long time has tried to pretend that priests were not human but some kind of super person. The result is that we appear to many both in and outside the church not to be more than human but less, ciphers, neuters, homeless freaks.

Celibacy does not mean that one does not fall in love or love; it rather means that one has made other commitments of such importance that one does not end up in bed with those one loves. Married men and women also fall in love; frequently it is with their spouse with whom they fall in love with all over again in one of the most delicious of all human romances, that of rediscovering the beloved stranger. But other times their loves, often sudden and transient, often profound and durable, are not their spouses. Yet infidelity usually does not occur and indeed is unthinkable because the basic commitments of their lives are richer, more important and more rewarding. To pretend that such reactions do not occur is absurd. To pretend that they are not possible is cynical and ugly.

One of the principle reasons for having celibates in a community is to have living proof that intense human emotional attractions need not end up in the bedroom and indeed need not even present a serious threat of doing so. The research finding that celibate confidants can play a special role in strengthening the marital satisfaction between a man and woman is, I believe, based not on the fact that the priest has special things to say to the wife, but on the fact that he is a special kind of person for her - his existence opens up new possibilities in her marriage. Far from being a non-erotic person, the good priest is a powerful erotic person in a community. Priests and laity would be a lot better off and a lot happier if they could admit it. Those who are not Catholic would understand a lot more about the nature of human nature if they could permit themselves to see it.

So, yeah, I have been in love often, sometimes for many years. Yet I have other commitments which are not really disturbed by such love and in fact are probably strengthened.

Are the persons who so attract me unappealing as bed partners? Heavens no, they grow more appealing through the years and the decades (an interesting discovery, by the way). Has the fact that they are not bed partners and won't be caused some frustration? Well, yes, but then the opposite outcome would have produced its own variety of frustrations, as married people will surely testify. All love has its frustrations and its rewards.

The point is, however, that there is a wide variety of possible loves available to humans, all of them with their own rewards, challenges, excitements, frustrations and disappointments. We cannot have them all, we must pick and choose.

The reason for having around a celibate who is both faithful and loving is that h/she stands as evidence of the variety, the possibility and the choice (Greeley, 1983, 129-131).

VI. METAPHYSICS

34. Introductory Thought: Alien Abductions

Many people, perhaps all of us, are consciously aware that there is something more to the world than what we perceive. There is an underlying reality that we want to make contact with.

- Paul Bloom

I realized I could not figure out the origin of these bizarre stories, nor could I prove or disprove the existence of aliens. Instead, I wanted to explore the human drama: who are these people, what has happened to them, and why does this distinguished Harvard professor believe them?

- Lauren Chiten, documentary filmmaker, "Touched"

One of the distinctions in the distinguished career of the late John Mack is that he is the only professor in the history of Harvard University to be considered for revocation of tenure. A *phi beta kappa* student, *cum laude* graduate of Harvard Medical School, Pulitzer Prize recognized author, medical school professor, and clinical psychiatrist, Dr. Mack ran afoul of his academic colleagues when his curiosity about alien abductions led him to interview 200 *alien abductees* (individuals who claim to have been taken by extraterrestrial beings, subjected to physical examination, and returned to the site of their abduction). When a number of Mack's fellow professors and others expressed concern about his research, a committee was appointed by the Dean of the Medical School to investigate the project.

Ostensibly, the investigation was intended to determine if his research was, in any way, harmful to the participants. Some of Dr. Mack's critics expressed concern that he was indulging the psychotic episodes of people who needed psychiatric treatment. However, much of the criticism of his study implied that Mack was engaged in research unbecoming for a Harvard scholar.

The committee's deliberation on the matter of alien abductee research raised the same question asked by Margery Williams' Velveteen Rabbit: "What is real?" (1986, 12). Mack's detractors, and are there were many, had concluded *a priori* that since there are no aliens it follows that anyone who claims to have been whisked away by them is either knowingly lying or delusional. Dr. Mack countered that such reasoning constituted *begging the question* (taking for granted an answer to the question being pursued). In defense of his curiosity, he argued as a psychiatrist with years of clinical experience, it was obvious to him that the subjects (also referred to as *experiencers*) were not psychotic. They were troubled by what they believe had happened to them, some even fearing they had lost their minds. Such apprehension is not characteristic of psychosis. In addition, similarities of the details of the testimonies of subjects who had never been in contact with each other constituted convergent data that could not be dismissed.

When pressured from different quarters (academics, mental health professionals, and journalists) to admit the experiencers were in need of psychiatric care, Mack steadfastly refused.

Responding to the charge that he was accepting at face value the testimonies of emotionally disturbed people, he said: "Face value I wouldn't say. I take them seriously. I don't have a way to account for them" (Feeney, 2004). Attempting to account for their experiences, he offered a tentative, metaphysical explanation. He theorized a dimension of reality peripheral to the material realm that occasionally, inexplicably crosses over. Perhaps, he suggested, this other dimension is inhabited by these mysterious beings. If a spiritual dimension is fit for consideration, he asked, why not a third realm that is neither physical nor spiritual? Referring to the spiritual, Mack said the experiences of the abductees had similarities to the unsolicited, transcendent experiences of mystics and visionaries. A problem, he added, is transcendent experiences are incompatible with the Western materialistic paradigm.

John Mack was killed on September 27, 2004. Crossing a street in London, England, he was hit by a car driven by a drunken driver. It is not surprising that no one at Harvard or any other academic institution has carried on his research. Hence, the investigations of alien abductions and second and third dimensions of reality remain unadvanced.

The philosopher Peter Kreeft has rightly observed that the scientific method requires that all ideas are "guilty until proven innocent" (2010, 69). John Mack's critics would say that he was in violation of this principle. To the contrary, his research was driven by his unwillingness to arbitrarily declare "innocent" the ideas that alien abductions and other dimensions of reality are fantasies - mental inventions indicative of psychosis

We inhabit a material world; is there a spiritual realm? Does God exist? Is there an afterlife existence for human beings? Is the universe eternal or was it created? If it was created, who or what created it and for what purpose, if any? These are philosophical questions of a specific type - *metaphysical*. The term metaphysics derives from two Greek words: *meta* ("after") and *phusikos* ("physical"). Aristotle hypothesized that if all questions concerning the material universe were answered another realm for investigation would remain - the nonphysical realm.

There are four stories in this chapter; each has a metaphysical component: An elderly woman lives with two corpses in her home. Albert Einstein is asked by a sixth grader if scientists pray. A baseball player's several brushes with death suggest divine protection. A surgeon wonders if his patient's healing was a miracle. (Malikow)

35. AFTERLIFE POSSIBILITIES

But that the dread of something after death,
The undiscovered country from whose born
No traveller returns, puzzles the will,
And makes us rather bear those ills we have
Than fly to others that we know not of
Thus conscience does make cowards of us all.

- Hamlet, 3.1

It is not rational arguments, but emotions, that cause belief in a future life.

- Bertrand Russell

It has been said that we all grieve in our own way. However, perhaps no one has ever grieved quite the same as Jean Stevens.

> **Wyalusing, PA** The 91-year-old widow lived by herself in a tumbledown house on a desolate country road. But she wasn't alone, not really, not as long as she could visit her husband and sister.
>
> No matter they were already dead. Jean Stevens simply had their embalmed corpses dug up and stored them at her house - in the case of her late husband, for more than a decade - tending to the remains as best she could until police were finally tipped off last month (Rubenkam, 2010).

"Death is very hard for me to take," admitted Mrs. Stevens. "I think that when you put them in the (ground), that's goodbye. Referring to her twin sister June, she said, "This way I could touch her and look at her and talk to her" (Rubinkam, 2010). (Certainly, maintaining corpses at home is eccentric behavior, to say the least. However, an interesting question to ponder is: If keeping dead bodies at home is bizarre, why is it culturally acceptable to keep at home cremated remains in an urn?)

An epitaph in a cemetery in Scotland reads:

> Consider friend, as you pass by, as you are now so once was I. As I am now, you too shall be. Prepare, therefore, to follow me

> (Myers, 2007, 187).

The process of a human body's decomposition is a matter for science. What one believes about the afterlife is a matter of faith. Where is this one whose epitaph speaks from the grave? Like John Brown, his or her body lies mouldering in the grave. Still, does the deceased have an existence in another form outside the scope of space, time, and the physical? This is the *afterlife question*. Although it cannot be answered definitively, it is a source of undying curiosity among the living. Sigmund Freud wrote of this curiosity in the essay, "On Transience:"

> ... to psychologists mourning is a great riddle, one of those phenomenon which cannot be explained ... why it is that this detachment of libido (capacity for love) from its objects should be such a painful process is a mystery to us and we have not ... been able to frame any hypothesis to account for it (1916, 178-179).

The remainder of this essay addresses the afterlife question to the extent that it can be considered analytically. Each of the six afterlife philosophical options is briefly described without any indication of logical superiority. (As previously stated, whatever one believes about the afterlife emerges from faith, not logic and certainly not empirical fact.)

The six possibilities are presented in alphabetical order as part of an effort to preclude any hint of the author's preference.

Agnosticism

Often associated with belief in God, *agnosticism* derives from the Greek words *a* ("without") and *gnosis* ("knowledge"). Related to death, the agnostic claims to be without knowledge concerning the after-life. Hamlet's soliloquey, in which he contemplates suicide, includes an agnostic statement where he speaks of death as the "undiscovered country" that "puzzles the will" (Shakespeare, circa 1600). Agnostics, in confessing ignorance concerning the afterlife, offer no speculation about the state of the deceased.

Annihilation

A little boy ran from his room looking for his mother. When he found her he asked, "Mom, is it true what they taught us in Sunday school: That we are made from dust and when we die we become dust again?

"Yes," said his mother, "in Genesis 3:19 it says, 'from dust we came and to dust we shall return.'"

With that the boy announced, "You better come look under my bed, because somebody's coming or somebody's going!"

Annihilationists believe that the dust under the bed is all that remains after death - physically and in every other way. The term itself literally means "to nothing" (Latin). Annihilation is a *monistic* view since it reflects the belief that reality has one constituent - the physical. Hence, human self-consciousness is contained within a functioning brain and when it ceases functioning self-awareness comes to an irreversible conclusion. Physicist and author Stephen Hawking unambiguously dismissed the notion of life after death with these words:

> I regard the brain as a computer which will stop
> working when its components fail. There is no
> heaven or afterlife for broken-down computers.

That is a fairy story for people afraid of the dark (2011, 9).

A second form of annihilationism associated with divine judgment is the belief that a benevolent God would not sentence anyone to a place of eternal suffering. Those who are appraised as unfit for heaven are annihilated; their punishment being the end of their existence.

Divine Judgment

This afterlife view requires belief in three conditions: a post-mortem form of existence; a relationship between one's earthly life and afterlife circumstance; and a being (God) to determine the afterlife circumstance. The concept of eternity in or away from God's abiding place constitute heaven or hell, respectively. This concept is associated with, but not limited to, evangelical Christianity. (Islam teaches this afterlife view, as well.)

Illusion

The oddest of the afterlife beliefs is held by practitioners of Christian Science, an organization founded by Mary Baker Eddy in 1866. Formally named the First Church of Christ Science, its followers believe that healing and health can be attained through prayer, study, and meditation, making medical treatment unnecessary. The textbooks of Christian Science are the *Bible* and *Science and Health with Key to the Scriptures* (Eddy, 1875). In the latter it is taught that illness and its ultimate manifestation, death, are illusions. The logic of this position is:

> God is the perfect Creator.
> All that God has created is perfect.
> All imperfections are false notions.
> Illness and death are imperfections.
> Therefore, illness and death are illusions.

Of course, this is such a bizarre doctrine that it is difficult to believe that it is a part of anyone's belief system. Nevertheless, not only is it found in Christian Science literature, but the foundation for this belief is recited at every service: "There is no life, truth, intelligence, nor substance in matter ... Spirit is the real and eternal; matter is the unreal and temporal" (Eddy, 468). Indeed, it is a rare afterlife position. Perhaps held only by Christian Scientists and probably not all of them.

Reincarnation

Reincarnation is the Western term for what Hindus and Buddhists speak of as *transmigration of the soul*. It is the afterlife belief that after death the immaterial soul inhabits another body, initiating a new life on earth. The appeal of this position is the necessity of many lives to attain the enlightenment necessary for living life as it ought to be lived. In psychiatrist Gordon Livingston's bestseller, *Too Soon Old, Too Late Smart*, he posits that by the time enough wisdom is accumulated for living a good life, life is nearly over (2004, 1-5). Reincarnation addresses this tragic irony with the reassurance that we have many lives to amass wisdom and enjoy its benefits.

Universalism

A 1969 hit song included the words: "I can swear that ain't no heaven, but I pray there ain't no hell" (Blood, Sweat, and Tears, 2011). Universalism is the afterlife belief that there is no hell and not only is there a heaven, but everyone goes there. The logic supporting this position is God's unfathomable love and infinite capacity to forgive. Concerning the latter, ultimately, even the most accomplished of evildoers cannot sin beyond God's forgiveness; neither can they resist His love for them.

Conclusion

The afterlife is a metaphysical issue, just as the start of all things is a metaphysical topic. Although neither the afterlife question nor the question of the origin of the universe can be answered, both are sub-jects of unending wonderment. Philosophers have pondered these questions more than most people, but all people have given them some thought. (Malikow)

36. Do Scientists Pray?

Strange is our situation on the earth. Each of us is here for a short time, sometimes seeming to divine a purpose.

- Albert Einstein

Albert Einstein fled from Germany in 1933 when the Nazis came to power. One can only wonder what Adolf Hitler would have decided to do about Einstein, a brilliant scientist and a Jew. As he became increasingly associated with science and genius, his opinion was sought out by people from all walks of life. A collection of letters from children includes a letter from Phyllis Wright, a sixth grader, who asked him if scientists pray (Einstein, 1936).

Dear Phyllis,

I have tried to respond to your question as simply as I could. Here is my answer.

Scientific research is based on the idea that everything that takes place is determined by the laws of nature, and therefore this holds for the actions of people. For this reason, a research scientist will hardly be inclined to believe that events could be influenced by a prayer, i.e. by a wish addressed to a supernatural Being.

However, it must be admitted that our actual knowledge of these laws is only imperfect and fragmentary, so that, actually, the belief in the existence of basic all-embracing laws in Nature also rests on a sort of faith. All the same this faith has been largely justified so far by the process of scientific research.

But, on the other hand, everyone who is seriously involved in the pursuit of science becomes convinced that a spirit is manifest in the laws of the Universe - a spirit vastly superior to that of man and one in the face of which we with our modest powers must feel humble. In this way the pursuit of science leads to a religious feeling of a special sort, which is quite indeed quite different from the religiosity of someone more naive.

I hope this answers your question.

Best wishes,
Yours
Albert Einstein

37. JACK "LUCKY" LOHRKE

Shortly before his death, baseball legend Lou Gehrig said, "I consider myself the luckiest man on the face of the earth." But it was a baseball player of less renown, Jack Lohrke, who had the nickname "Lucky." According to his son, John, "He really didn't like that nickname. It reminded him of too many things." Jack Lohrke didn't like being reminded of his several brushes with death.

"Because I could not stop for death, he kindly stopped for me," wrote Emily Dickinson (1924). Finally, at age 85, two days after suffering a stroke, death stopped for Jack Lohrke. A World War II veteran, he fought at Normandy and the Battle of the Bulge and emerged unscathed. Four times a soldier next to him was killed. He didn't consider himself a hero ("I wasn't exactly Sgt. York") any more than he considered himself lucky ("The name is Jack, Jack Lohrke") (Fimrite, 1994).

Returning home in 1945, he was bumped from a transport flight at the last minute. The plane crashed, killing everyone on board. The following year, having resumed his baseball career, Lohrke was traveling by bus in Washington state with a Class B minor league team, the Spokane Indians. During a stop for food, he was told he had been promoted to Triple A, so he took his gear and hitchhiked to Spokane. A few hours later the Indians' bus crashed into a canyon, killing nine of his former teammates.

Lohrke went on to a seven-year major league career with the New York Giants and Philadelphia Phillies, retiring with a career batting average of .242 and 22 home runs. He appeared as a pinch hitter in the 1951 World Series. Still, he is best remembered for surviving a war and two crashes that almost included him.

Fate is an irresistible power believed to control events. Luck is the unknown and unknowable means by which events happen. Is there a power that controls events and was Jack Lohrke favored by that power? If so, is the reason for this favor discoverable? Or, is it luck? (Malikow).

38. JOE RIKER

I don't dawdle. I'm a surgeon. I make an incision, do what needs to be done and sew up the wound. There is a beginning, a middle and an end.
- Richard Selzer, M.D.

The above quotation notwithstanding, Richard Selzer is not only a surgeon, he is a writer - an excellent one. The author of over a dozen books, almost all of his writing is about one subject: what it is like to be a doctor. The enigmatic case of Joe Riker is found in Dr. Selzer's Mortal Lessons: The Art of Surgery *(1974).*

What is to one man a coincidence is to another a miracle. It was one or the other of these that I saw last spring. While the rest of nature was in flux, Joe Riker remained obstinate through the change of seasons. "No operation," said Joe, "I don't want no operation."

Joe Riker is a short-order cook in a diner where I sometimes drink coffee. Each week for six months he has paid a visit to my office, carrying his affliction like a pet mouse under his hat. Every Thursday at four o'clock he would sit on my examination table, lift the fedora from his head, and bend forward to show me the hole. Joe Riker's hole was as big as his mouth. You could have dropped a plum in it. Gouged from the tonsured top of his head was a mucky puddle whose meaty heaped edge rose above the normal scalp around it. There was no mistaking the announcement from this rampart.

The cancer had chewed through Joe's scalp, munched his skull, then opened the membranes underneath - until it had laid bare this short-order cook's brain, pink and gray and pulsating so that with each beat a little pool of cerebral fluid quivered. Now and then a drop would manage the rim to run across his balding head, and Joe would reach one burry hand to wipe it away with the heel of his thumb, the way such a man would wipe a tear.

I would gaze then upon Jo Riker and marvel. How dignified he was, as though that tumor, gnawing him, denuding his very brain, had given him a grace that a lifetime of good health had not bestowed.

"Joe," I say, "let's get rid of it. Cut out the bad part, put in a metal plate, and you're cured." And I wait.

"No operation," says Joe. I try again.

"What do you mean, 'no operation'? You're going to get meningitis. Any day now. And die. That thing is going to get to your brain."

I think of it devouring the man's dreams and memories. I wonder what they are. The surgeon knows all the parts of the brain, but he does not know his patient's dreams and memories. His dreams are none of my business. It is his flesh that matters.

"No operation," says Joe.

"You give me a headache," I say. And we smile, not because the joke is funny anymore, but because we've got something between us, like a secret.

"Same time next week?" Joe asks. I wash out the wound with peroxide and apply a dressing. He lowers the fedora over it.

"Yes," I say, "same time." And the next week he comes again.

There came the week when Joe did not show up; nor did he the week after that; nor for a whole month. I drive over to his diner. He is behind the counter, shuffling back and forth between the grill and the sink. He is wearing the fedora. He sets a cup of coffee in front of me.

"I want to see your hole," I say.

"Which one?" he asks, and winks.

"Never mind that," I say, "I want to see it." And I am all business.

"Not here," says Joe. He looks around, checking the counter, as though I have made an indecent suggestion.

"My office at four o'clock," I say.

"Yeah," says Joe, and turns away.

He is late. Everyone has gone for the day. Joe is beginning to make me angry. At last he arrives.

"Take off your hat," I say, and he knows by my voice that I am not happy. He does, though, raise it straight up with both hands the way he always does, and I see ... that the wound has healed. Where once there had been a bitten-out excavation, moist and shaggy, there is now a fragile bridge of shiny new skin.

"What happened?" I manage.

"You mean that?" He points to the top of his head. "Oh well," he says, "the wife's sister, she went to France and bought me a bottle of water from Lourdes. I've been washing it out with that for a month."

"Holy water?" I say.

"Yeah," says Joe. "Holy water."

I see Joe now and then at the diner. He looks like anything but a fleshly garden of miracles. Rather, he has taken on a terrible ordinariness. Eden, after the Fall, and minus its most beautiful creatures. There is a certain slovenliness, a dishevelment of the tissues. Did the disease ennoble him, and now that it is gone he is somehow diminished? Perhaps I am wrong. Perhaps the only change is the sly wink with which he greets me, as though to signal that we have shared something furtive. Could such a man, I think as I sip my coffee, could such a man have felt the brush of wings? How often it seems that the glory leaves as soon as the wound is healed. But then it is only saints who bloom in martyrdom, becoming less and less the flesh that pains, more and more ghost-colored weightlessness.

It was many years between my first sight of the living human brain and Joe Riker's windowing. I had thought then, long ago: Could this one-pound loaf of sourdough be the pelting brain? *This*, along whose circuitry run Reason and Madness in perpetual race - a race that often ends in a tie? But the look deceives. What seems a fattish snail drowsing in its shell, in fact lives in quickness, where all is dart and stir and rapids of electricity.

Once again to the operating room ... (Selzer, 27-29).

VII. FREE WILL AND RESPONSIBILITY

39. Introductory Thought: The Law of Unintended Consequences and Personal Responsibility

On December 6, 2006 in Syracuse, New York, a jury found twenty-one year-old James Carncross guilty of criminally negligent homicide in the death of Trooper Craig Todeschini. Eight months earlier Todeschini was killed when he lost control of his SUV while in pursuit of Carncross, who was on a motorcycle evading the trooper at speeds in excess of 100 miles per hour. A person has acted with criminal negligence when his or her action created a substantial and unjustified risk that an ordinary person would perceive as substantial and unjustified. The jury did not find Carncross guilty of manslaughter: the killing of another with neither premeditation nor intention to kill.

The trial of James Carncross raised a philosophical question that has reverberated through as many centuries as human beings have been thinking about their behavior: How is personal responsibility determined?

It is one thing to say – and this is indisputable – that we are responsible for our actions. Stated more precisely, we are responsible for the consequences of our actions. However, this is not to say that we are responsible for every event in a sequence that was initiated by something we have done. We are responsible for any and all foreseeable events that followed our actions and are connected to them. There is no formula for distinguishing foreseeable events from those that are unforeseeable. This is a matter of judgment.

The Law of Unintended Consequences maintains that every significant action is followed by unplanned events. Implicit in this law is that statements like, "I didn't intend for X to happen," and "I didn't anticipate that X would happen" are inadequate for the relief of responsibility. We are responsible for the intentions and imaginable effects of our behavior. Nevertheless, "I didn't mean or anticipate for X to happen" is not the same thing as saying, "I could not have imagined that X would happen."

Applying the Law of Unintended Consequences to this case, it is unreasonable to assume that Trooper Todeschini's death was one of the things James Carncross should have anticipated when he decided to take flight. It is doubtful that Carncross deliberated before attempting his escape. If he considered any possibilities, they would have included getting caught, getting away, or getting himself killed. To have anticipated Todeschini's death, Carncross would have had to calculate that the trooper had no alternative means of pursuit and would not break-off the chase – even if it meant pursuing in excess of the SUV's maneuvering capability. Ironically – some might say demonically – Carncross took for granted the trooper's high speed driving ability and good judgment in making pursuit. In other words, Carncross took for granted Todeschini's ability to take care of himself.

What is James Carncross responsible for in the events that culminated in the death of Trooper Todeschini? Unquestionably, Carncross is responsible for initiating the chase and, according to the jury, responsible for Todeschini's death. This was the finding of the jury, regardless of any poor judgment the trooper might have exercised in pursuit. The argument of the defense was that the accident was unforeseeable because the trooper was a professional trained in the pursuit of speeders. It was the argument of the prosecution that prevailed. The prosecution argued that even if the accident was unforeseeable, Carncross' high speed attempt to escape *created a substantial and unjustified risk that an ordinary person would perceive as substantial and unjustified.* (Malikow)

40. A MOMENT OF SHARED TRUST

No man is an island, entire of itself.

- John Donne

Warren Christopher served as President Clinton's Secretary of State. When Christopher died in March of 2011 the President's eulogy included these words: "Chris had the lowest ego-to-accomplishment ratio of any public servant I've ever worked with. ... I was honored by his service and enriched by his friendship" (Clinton, 2011, 26). In this essay, Christopher reflects on the deeper meaning of an everyday occurrence.

One night I was driving down a two-lane highway at about sixty miles an hour. A car approached from the opposite direction, at about the same speed. As we passed each other, I caught the other driver's eye for only a second.

I wondered whether he might be thinking, as I was, how dependent we were on each other at that moment. I was relying on him not to fall asleep, not to be distracted by a cell phone conversation, not to cross over into my lane and bring my life suddenly to an end. And though we had never spoken a word to one another, he relied on me in just the same way.

Multiplied a million times over, I believe that is the way the world works. At some level, we all depend upon one another. Sometimes that dependence requires us simply to refrain from doing something, like crossing over the double yellow line. And sometimes it requires us to act cooperatively, with allies or even with strangers.

Back in 1980, I was negotiating for the release of the fifty-two Americans held hostage in Iran. The Iranians refused to meet with me face-to-face, insisting instead that we send messages back and forth through the government of Algeria. I had never before worked with the Algerian foreign minister, I had to rely on him to receive and transmit, with absolute accuracy, both the words and the nuances of my messages. With his indispensable help, all fifty-two Americans came home safely.

As technology shrinks our world, the need increases for cooperative action among nations. In 2003, doctors in five nations were quickly mobilized to identify the SARS virus, an action that saved thousands of lives. The threat of international terrorism has shown itself to be a similar problem, one requiring coordinated action by police and intelligence forces across the world. We must recognize that our fates are not ours alone to control

In my own life, I've put great stock in personal responsibility. But, as the years have passed, I've also come to believe that there are moments when one must rely upon the good faith and judgment of others. So, while each of us faces - at one time or another - the prospect of driving alone down a dark road, what we must learn with experience is that the approaching light may not be a threat, but a shared moment of trust (Christopher, 2006).

41. Dr. Peck's Confession

Triggers are pulled by individuals. Orders are given and executed by individuals. In the last analysis, every single human act is ultimately the result of an individual choice.

- Scott Peck

We are all much less than we can be.

- Leonard Buscaglia

Sir Winston Churchill characterized the Soviet Union's foreign policy as "a puzzle inside a riddle wrapped in an enigma." This description also fits the celebrated psychiatrist and author Scott Peck. In his writing he emphasized the necessity and benefits of self-discipline. Yet, he admitted to a lack of restraint in his personal life. Whatever his faults, hypocrisy was not one of them. In one of his books he candidly confessed to three of his deficiencies and failures. This essay addresses the question: Does a confession constitute taking responsibility?

Published in 1978, Scott Peck's *The Road Less Traveled* did not become a bestseller until 1984. Eventually translated into twenty languages, over the next quarter century it sold over six million copies, making it the all-time bestselling nonfiction book with one exception - the *Bible*. He was listed in the *Guinness Book of World's Records* for having written the longest running book on the *New York Times* bestsellers list.

The Road Less Traveled begins with these three words: "Life is difficult" (1978,1). Peck proceeds to explain that life is difficult because it consists of a series of problems, which we can moan about or solve. He is optimistic about our predicament because it has a remedy.

> Discipline is the basic set of tools we need to solve life's problems. Without discipline we can solve nothing. With only some discipline we can solve only some problems. With total discipline we can solve all problems (1978,1-2).

Yet the same man who wrote these words also confessed to his failure to apply discipline in solving three problems in his own life: alcohol dependency, smoking, and marital infidelity. After reading Dr. Peck's confessions, consider whether or not they constitute an assumption of responsibility.

Alcohol

> I am strongly habituated to alcohol. I eagerly look forward to my gin in quite heavy doses at the end of a day. This habit has become more entrenched over the years. I dearly love the solace it brings me - the relaxation that results from having the edge taken off my consciousness - and I tend to adjust my day around the "cocktail hour" - or two or three hours (Peck, 1995, 43).

Smoking

> Without nicotine for a couple of waking hours I become sick. ... For over forty years now I have used smoking, somewhat like alcohol, to provide me with brief respites from concentration and rewards for periods of hard mental work. No work requires such intense concentration as writing, and if I ever kick this fierce addiction it will probably only be at a time when I have ceased to write anymore (42-43).

Adultery

My sexual infidelity is a glaring example of the unreasonableness of romance. I would never have been diagnosed as a full-blown "sex addict," but in some ways it was surely a compulsion. A purely rational human being would have known better. I, however, am not purely rational, and this irrational part of me had to have its due. I might not have survived otherwise, but I always wished I could have been a different kind of person who did not need such an outlet. ... Extramarital sex is ... a new body and a new personality to be explored. A new territory. It is also forbidden territory, and for some that might be a turn-on. For me it never was. Whatever my psychology, the pure newness of another woman was my primary aphrodisiac (28-30).

Is Making a Confession Tantamount to Taking Responsibility?

It is easier to recognize a confession than determine whether or not responsibility has been taken. To confess is to admit to the truth of something. Taking responsibility is more complicated. A confession takes the form: "If not for me, X would not have happened." An expansion to this statement is required for the assumption of responsibility: "Because of X, Y happened. Therefore, I am responsible for both X and Y."

A further complication in determining responsibility occurs when Y is not foreseeable. In the case of Dr. Peck's adultery, consider this hypothetical: *What if his wife, Lily, committed suicide after learning of his extramarital affairs?* Would Peck be responsible for her death? Should it be assumed that as a well-trained, experienced psychiatrist he could have predicted her suicide? (Not all women betrayed in this way kill themselves.) In addition, if her husband's philandering was "the last straw," is he responsible for the aggregate of straws that preceded his unfaithfulness?

The *law of unintended consequences* provides another complicating factor. It posits that every action is followed by unanticipated subsequent events. While this law might seem to provide some relief of responsibility, it could be argued that anyone aware of it is culpable for unforeseeable events as well. In other words, even if it is impossible to know *all* events that will follow an action, this unpredictability should be taken into account before acting. Since we cannot know the extent and nature of the ripple effect of our behaviors, we have an obligation to be confident of the propriety of our actions before taking them. To return to the Lily hypothetical, even if her suicide could not be predicted, Dr. Peck conceded to the wrongfulness of his adultery.

There is no relaxation of responsibility owing to unintentionality or designating an action as a "necessary evil." For instance, with President Harry Truman's decision to drop atomic bombs over Hiroshima and Nagasaki came his responsibility for the collateral damage of civilian fatalities, many of them children. To his credit, Truman did not rationalize that he was not responsible for these deaths since his intention was to end the war and the bombings were a necessary evil for accomplishing that end.

Again, returning to Lily's suicide, it is reasonable to ask, "Is she not responsible for her decision to end her life?" If so, her husband's serial adultery may have been influential, but it was not coercive. This would make her suicide an instance of unquantifiable shared responsibility.

Given these several considerations, Dr. Peck seems to have taken responsibility for his addictions and adultery. He pointed to no other person or condition as the explanation for any of his behaviors. He suggested nothing that diluted his exercise of free will. He characterized his smoking, drinking, and womanizing as volitional. In his authorized biography, published two years after his death, he refers to these habits as freely chosen and views Lily's decision to divorce him as the result of his own doing (Jones, 2007).

Postscript

If it is true that Scott Peck took responsibility for the behaviors he confessed, his son was not favorably impressed. Shortly after Dr. Peck's death, his son Christopher offered the analysis that his father was not a Jekyll and Hyde character,

> ... because Jekyll and Hyde split himself into vice and virtue, but Scotty's virtue was really a sham. His narcissism left him a very lonely person, and his saintliness (which I found creepier than his cruelty) was a plea for love. I don't think he loved because he enjoyed loving others; he loved in order to be loved back (274).

Concerning Peck's relationships with his children, Arthur Jones, Peck's biographer, wrote:

> Peck was indeed deeply regretting his extremely troubled relationships with his three children. Perversely, he couldn't, or rather wouldn't, admit the extent to which he was responsible for the fissures and faults that had caused the breech. An unparalleled wordsmith in conversation, he was unable or unwilling to express remorse sufficient to the damage done, in words that sincerely conveyed what he felt or ought to have felt (268).

A "light bulb" joke that circulated a few years ago might provide some insight into the unfortunate state of Peck's relationships with his wife and children. *Question: How many psychiatrists does it take to change a light bulb? Answer: Only one, but the light bulb has to really want to change.* A lawsuit or criminal action can assign responsibility, produce a sentence (imprisonment and/or fine), but cannot compel change. The determination to not repeat a behavior must come from the individual. In personal matters, especially among people whose lives are intertwined, injured parties expect offenders to make an unfeigned effort at change. It is understandable that those hurt by another's misbehavior want reassurance that the behavior will not be repeated. They have the implicit assumption and hope that taking responsibility includes a commitment to change. In the movie "A Civil Action," victims of irresponsible industrial waste disposal are told that the perpetrators, "Say they're sorry with money" (Touchstone, 1998). Dissatisfied with the offer of an eight million dollar settlement, the victims insist on *change*. They want the contaminated water wells cleansed and dumping practices discontinued. They are disappointed and bewildered by the offending corporation's simultaneous confession of wrongdoing and refusal to change.

In the *New Testament*, the Apostle Paul wrote to Christian believers at Corinth, "Godly sorrow worketh repentance" (2 Corinthians 7:10). This teaching communicates the insufficiency of mere confession in the Christian life. Paul adjures those to whom he has written that in order for confession to be meaningful it must be accompanied by a determined effort to discontinue the behavior. This commitment to change is captured by the Greek word *metanoia*, translated in the English *New Testament* as *repent*. *Metanoia* is a marching term meaning "about face," that is, "turn around and walk in the opposite direction."

It appears that Peck resigned himself to three unwanted behaviors. While he didn't rationalize them, he explained them, thereby demonstrating that an etiological understanding of a behavior is insufficient to effect change. Certain is that he did not repent in the strictest (*metanoia*) sense of the word. Dr. Peck's condition is far from unique; it is recognizable to many who are plagued, if not tormented, with unwanted behaviors. For them it is small consolation that making confession is tantamount to taking responsibility since neither is sufficient for change. (Malikow)

42. DWI Prevention, Not Penalty

Drinking and driving: there are stupider things, but the list is very short.
- Unknown

The best automobile safety device is a rear view mirror, with a cop in it.
- Dudley Moore

Rhetoric is the use of language to influence the thoughts and actions of listeners. Tom Anelli is founder of the law firm Anelli Xavier, P.C., a statewide DWI defense firm located in Syracuse, New York. What is your estimation of the quality of his persuasive argument in this essay that appeared in a newspaper's editorial page?

DWI is a crime. However, DWI is a crime people commit when their cognitive ability is impaired by alcohol.

Some individuals struggle with alcohol addictions, making them more likely to be charged with DWI. Others misjudge their level of intoxication before driving.

For these reasons, laws created stiffer penalties when individuals are caught driving drunk do little to prevent individuals from driving drunk in the first place.

Also, unless individuals are reading law books or watching the news, which aren't common behaviors of most charged with DWI, they don't learn about the stiffer penalty until after they are charged.

Isn't it far better to take some measures to stop drunk driving before it occurs?

As a consequence of what I do, I see the life-altering negative affects of DWI, day in and day out. So, please understand, I am not minimizing the responsibility of individuals to drive sober or not at all, if they have had drinks.

That being said, let's take a look at what we know:

We know in certain sections of the city, and at certain events, drinking to the point of intoxication is foreseeable (i.e. bar districts, concerts, etc.).

We know when these events occur and when people will be leaving them.

We know events (Super Bowl) and holidays (St. Patrick's Day) are promoted around drinking.

We know cities have bar districts where Thursday, Friday, and Saturday nights people leave intoxicated between the hours of 11 p.m. and 3 a.m.

We know hundreds if not thousands of individuals will be driving, or at least be tempted to drive drunk on these days, at these hours, and from these locations.

Why do we not provide convenient alternative transportation?

Are we serious about the problem of drunk driving? I would submit we are not.

Few of the bar districts have convenient alternative transportation.

Few events are planned to provide convenient alternative transportation.

Instead we sit back and say, "shame on you drunk drivers, you should have known better."

We expect a 20-year-old to make the right decision and not drive after they have had too much to drink, rather than providing them with a convenient acceptable alternative.

Shouldn't we expect those in charge of our cities to provide convenient alternative transportation in areas and at times where drunk patrons are foreseeable?

Wouldn't we support a slight increase in taxes to support such a goal?

Here's my take on it. When we as communities are serious about the problem of drunk driving, convenient alternative transportation will be provided.

Until then, the problem of drunk driving and the statistics relative to the same will be unfazed by laws like O'Shea's Law, Leandra's Law and the advent of intoxalock devices.

I submit prevention, my friends, works far better than penalty (Anelli, 2010).

43. INTOLERABLE
INDIGNITIES

The law is reason free from passion.

- Aristotle

Gravitation is not responsible for people falling in love.

- Albert Einstein

*It is understandable that Gerry Spence is one of America's most celebrated trial lawyers. He is renown for never having lost a criminal case decided by a jury. His high-profile clients included Imelda Marcos, Karen Silkwood, and Randy Weaver. In addition, he was successful in a $52 million lawsuit against Mc Donald's and a $26 million lawsuit against Penthouse Magazine. In addition, he is a bestselling author (*How to Argue and Win Every Time*, 1995).*

In the following excerpt from his autobiography, The Making of a Country Lawyer *(1996), he confesses his ambivalence over divorcing his wife, Anna, in order to marry the woman of his passion, Imaging. One would think that a man who made a career of defending the accused and successfully persuading juries to find "not guilty" would have felt less guilty about his divorce.*

Invited or not, I received constant advice from my friends. One friend was Charles Hamilton, a Riverton lawyer whose father had been dean of the Wyoming Law School, a man who had been important in helping me make my early decisions. The younger Hamilton rented space from me in my new small office building. One day he sat down with me to convince me that I should go home to Anna. He listed all the reasons why.

"This falling in love is bullshit," Hamilton said. "You are thinking with your dick. When your dick goes down, this love thing will wear off, but maybe it'll be too late. Maybe you'll go home, and Anna and the kids won't be there anymore." He began writing on a napkin the reasons why I should stay with Anna. I already knew them.

Anna is the mother of your children.

She's a good woman.

You will never get over the guilt.

You have never lived a day with Imaging - how do you know it will work?

You will hurt your children beyond repair.

Statistically, second marriages don't work.

You are crazy. (How can a crazy man make an intelligent decision that will irrevocably affect the lives of his wife and four kids?)

You are not sure. (If you were sure, you wouldn't be in such a miserable quandary.)

Besides, going home is the *right* thing to do.

... More and more I fell into the extravagant phases of manic depression. With Imaging I was wildly happy. Without her I wallowed in the deepest abyss. Often I wondered about my mother. Was this the pain she had experienced? ...

My divorce from Anna had been one of those default affairs in an empty courtroom, all the property and custody issues having been previously worked out by the lawyers, the assets split down the middle. When my case was called up, I sat there on the witness stand in an empty courtroom with Bob Rose, by then my (law) partner, asking the questions, the judge looking down, nobody else giving a damn. In Wyoming you had to establish fault - "intolerable indignities" was the test. You took the oath, and then you testified to something against your spouse, the indignities which had supposedly rendered the marriage intolerable.

"What has happened in your marriage that has made it intolerable?" Rose asked the standard question. I thought for a long time. The judge waited.

> *Falling in love when you're tied to another,*
> *Yeah baby, fallin' in love when you're tied to another,*
> *Is like fallin' to the bottom of a well, my brother.*

I thought of jumping up and hollering, "I've fallen in love with another woman, Your Honor. And that renders the marriage intolerable for everybody. You have been there yourself, Your Honor," and he had. I thought of saying, "What is intolerable is watching Anna fight to hold on to her family. You cannot imagine the pain - for both of us." Nothing would come. Then I wept. And after a while the judge broke through it.

"You want a divorce?" the judge finally asked.

I nodded. I couldn't look up.

"Divorce granted," he said, and he walked off the bench.

That was 1969, and within days after my divorce, Imaging and I had run off to Tahoe to get married. I used to laugh about it - just as well - that I've been unmarried only nine days in my entire adult life. The Sunday morning shrinks would have said I had escaped one trap only to fall into another. But a trap of love is not a trap. It's heaven with a fence around it. Imaging changed my life. ...

"We gotta make this thing work, Imaging," I said. "If we don't we've screwed ourselves good."

"And everybody else," she said. If love meant anything it had to be responsible - we said things like that. I knew the booze was in the way. She knew it, too. The booze was dangerous, it had to go.

... we celebrated our marriage with a couple of hot fudge sundaes at Zim's.

"Here's to us," I said. I held up a dripping spoonful of ice cream and chocolate.

I'll eat to that," Imaging said holding up her own dripping spoon ...

"Strange life without the booze, like losing an old friend," I said.

"We have to find new friends. If you aren't drunk with your old friends you can't stand'em anymore," Imaging said. "Sometimes I look in the bars now," she said. "You know, when you walk from the dining room and see in, and you see all the losers lined up at the bar."

"I used to hang in the bars with all the losers. I was a loser," I said. ...

I used to say to a friend who was laying the guilt on himself that guilt was the handiest self-flagellator I knew. "You wouldn't whip a friend like you whip yourself," I'd say. "But when it's you, you flog yourself unmercifully with the guilt whip, and you suffer. Then one day you've whipped yourself enough, and you know it. May take years, but one day you wake up and out of the blue you say, 'I've had enough. I've punished myself enough. This atonement is over. You, Guilt, get your ass out of here!'" And one day that's what I said. I said, "Guilt, get your ass out of here. I've had enough of you." And I had. But once in a while the demon snuck back in (Spence, 1996, 419-420).

44. PATHOLOGICAL GAMBLING

I realize that nothing in the world is more distasteful to a man than to take the path that leads him to himself.

- Herman Hesse

During the late 1980's, the sports world was shaken by the story that one of the leading baseball figures of all time, Pete Rose, had been betting thousands of dollars a day on baseball games. Admitting his guilt, Rose publicly acknowledged that he was unable to control his gambling, despite his realization that this would lead to his banishment from baseball. Pete Rose's problem brought attention to a disorder with which few Americans were familiar (Halgin and Whitbourne, 2000, 435).

The issue of responsibility is writ large in the story of Arelia Taveras. In assessing responsibility for her situation, consider that brain research has shown there is a neurological component to compulsive gambling. Also consider her claim that casinos are responsible to "cut-off" gamblers just as bars are responsible to not serve customers who are intoxicated.

Taveras, a disbarred New York City attorney, was sentenced May 6, 2009 to three to nine years in prison for embezzling $130,000 from her clients' accounts. She stole the money to finance her gambling. Queens District Attorney Richard A. Brown said Taveras "violated the trust of her clients and let down the entire legal system, which counts on members of the bar to conduct themselves in an ethical manner" (Associated Press, 05/27/2009).

Taveras previously had filed a $20 million federal lawsuit against six Atlantic City casinos and one in Las Vegas, claiming casino employees knew she was a compulsive gambler but did nothing to stop her from accumulating nearly $1 million in losses. She said she often gambled for days a a time and at least twice passed out while playing, only to resume as soon as she came to.

> They knew I was going for days without eating or sleeping. I would pass out at the tables. They had a duty of care to me. Nobody in their right mind would gamble for four or five straight days without sleeping (TPI News, 03/09/2008).

The casinos denied any wrongdoing, claiming their employees were not responsible for Taveras' behavior and the problems that followed it. The suit was dismissed and her appeal rejected because she hadn't paid the required court fees.

The refrain of Kenny Rogers' popular song, "The Gambler," contains the lesson Arelia Taveras was unable to actualize: "You've got to know when to hold 'em, know when to fold 'em. Know when to walk away; know when to run" (Schlitz, 1978). She was not alone in her failure to walk away; Edgar Allen Poe and Fyodor Dostoevsky also were pathological gamblers. Dostoevsky wrote his novella, *The Gambler*, to generate income to offset his gambling losses (1997). Using Dostoevsky as a case study, Sigmund Freud analyzed the author's gambling as self-punishing behavior emanating from unresolved Oedipal guilt. (Malikow)

45. WHAT IS A MISTAKE?

In June of 2011 United States Congressman Anthony Weiner (Democrat, New York) admitted to sending lewd photos of himself to several women. His admission came two days after publicly denying having done so. Confessing at a press conference, he referred to sending the explicit pictures and subsequent lying as "mistakes." Weiner's use of the word "mistake" in this context is, at least, questionable.

Think about the word "mistake." Legally, "a mistake occurs when a person believes a condition to exist when it does not." A dictionary definition of "mistake" is, "to understand wrongly or identify incorrectly."

Consider two events that fit these definitions. (1) Walking through a shopping mall, you spot a friend walking in front of you. Calling your friend's name, you accelerate your pace. When you catch up, your "friend" turns out to be someone else. You've made a "mistake!" (2) Running late for work, you pick up your car keys. You later discover that in your haste you picked up your spouse's keys. You've made a "mistake!"

Since a "mistake" is the unintentional, unaware belief that something is true when it isn't, it's obvious that Congressman Weiner misappropriated the word "mistake" when he referred to his electronic messaging and subsequent lying as "mistakes." I suggest the following phrases as more descriptive of his behavior: "moral failure," "moral lapse," "suspension of wisdom," "morally questionable judgment," and either "action out of character" or "defining episode." Each of these phrases implies intentionality, which is necessary for taking responsibility.

Anyone inclined to respond to what I've written with the adage, "Judge not, lest ye be judged," should admit that characterizing Mr. Weiner's behavior as a "mistake" is no less a judgment.

Of course, the Congressman could say that his use of the word "mistake" was a "mistake."

(Malikow)

REFERENCES

Preface

Katen, T. (1973). *Doing philosophy*. Englewood Cliffs, New Jersey: Prentice - Hall.

Introduction

James, W. (1907) "The present dilemma of philosophy." *Pragmatism*. New York: Longman Green and Company.

Miller, E. (1992). *Questions that matter: An invitation to philosophy*. New York: McGraw-Hill, Inc.

I. Epistemology

Adler, M. (1980). *How to think about God*. New York: Touchstone/Simon and Schuster.

Carroll, A., Editor. (1997). *Letters of a nation*. New York: Broadway Books.

Descartes, R. (2004). *The principles of philosophy*. Kila, MT: Kissinger Publishing.

Freud, S. (1961). *The future of an illusion*. translated by Strachey, J. New York: W.W. Norton & Company Ltd.

Johnson, S. (2005). *Everything bad is good for you: How today's popular culture is actually making us smarter*. New York: Riverhead Books.

Kohn, A. (2004). *What does it mean to be well educated?* Boston, MA: Beacon Press.

Malikow, M. (2010). *Being human: Philosophical reflections on psychological issues.* Lanham, MD: Rowman and Littlefield Publishing Group.

Meier, D. (1995). *The power of their ideas.* Boston, MA: Beacon Press.

Plato. (1968). *The republic of Plato.* (translated by Allan Bloom). New York: Basic Books.

Rose, R. (1954). *12 angry men.* New York: Penguin Classics.

Wallace, D. (2009). *This is water: Some thoughts delivered on a significant occasion, about living a compassionate life.* New York: Little, Brown, and Company.

II. Logic

Dershowitz, A. Permission to reprint this essay was given by Alan Dershowitz on 12/26/2010.

Kreeft, P. (1993). *The unaborted Socrates.* Downers Grove, IL: InterVarsity Press.

Malikow, M. "Did the jury reach a decision that Oswego caseworkers did not?" The Syracuse Post Standard. August 14, 2009.

Parsons, R. "Towing over parking violation was excessive." The Syracuse Post Standard. September 19, 2007.

Szasz, T. (1973). *The myth of metal illness.* New York: HarperCollins.

vos Savant, M. (1997). *The power of logical thinking: Easy lessons in the art of thinking … and hard facts about its absence in our lives.* New York: St. Martins Griffen.

Whyte, J. (2004). *Crimes against logic: Exposing the bogus arguments of politicians, priests, journalists, and other serial offenders.* New York: McGraw - Hill.

III. Ethics

Allport, G.W. & Odbert, H.S. (1936). "Trait names: A psycho-lexical study." *Psychological monographs: general and applied,* 47, 171 - 220. (1, Whole No. 211).

American heritage dictionary. (1973). New York: American Heritage Publishing Company.

Barkley, C. www.brainyquotes.com. Recovered 12/25/10.

Baum, L.F. (2000). *The wizard of Oz:* 100th anniversary edition. New York: HarperCollins.

Bloom, A. (1987). *The closing of the American mind.* New York: Touchstone/Simon and Schuster.

Bok, S. (1978). Lying: *Moral choice in public and private life.* New York: Random House.

Bunnell, D. (1974). "Tin Man." America (recording group).

Cabot, M. (2008). *The princess diaries.* New York: Harper Teen.

Carson, B. (2006). "There is no job more important than parenting." *This i believe: The personal philosophies of remarkable men and women.* New York: Henry Holt and Company.

Chesterton, G.K. recovered from www.quote/quotes/839 on 10/21/2010.

Dostoevsky, F. (1970). *The brothers Karamazov,* translated A.H. MacAndrew New York: Bantam, 1970.

Deveney, K. "Liar, liar, parents on fire." Newsweek. 04/07/2008.

Fagone, J. Philadelphia Magazine. 5/15/2006.

Frankl, V. (1959). *Man's search for meaning.* New York: Washington Square Books.

Freud, S. (1989). *Civilization and its discontents.* New York: W.W. Norton and Company.

Geisel, T. 1954. *Horton hears a who.* New York: Random House.

Gibbs, N. "Pillow angel ethics." Time. January 22, 2007. 56-57.

Haidt, J. 2006. *The happiness hypothesis: Finding modern truth in ancient wisdom.* New York: Basic Books.

Hammond, A. & Bettis, J. (1988). "One moment in time." Houston, W. (recording artist).

Hartsock, D. "Couric & Company." CBSnews.com. May 10, 2010 (interview).

Homer. (1998). *The iliad.* Fagles, R. (translator).New York: Penguin Classics.

Hornby, N. (2001). *How to be good.* New York: Riverhead Books.

Hugo, V. (1987). *Les miserables.* New York: Penguin Books: Signet Classic.

James, W. (1907). "The present dilemma of philosophy." *Pragmatism.* New York: Longman Green and Company.

_____ (1902) *Varieties of religious experience.* New York: Touchstone Publishers.

Jamison, K. (1995). *An unquiet mind: A memoir of moods and madness.* New York: Randon House, Inc.

Johnson, T.L. (2007). *The Teaching Company.* Chantilly, VA.

Kelly, N. Quoted from an interview conducted on 03/18/2011.

Kilpatrick, W.K. (1993). *Why Johnny can't tell right from wrong.* New York: Simon and Schuster.

Kohlberg, L. (1984). *The psychology of moral development: Essays on moral development* (Vol. 2). San Francisco: Harper and Row.

Kreeft, P. (2007). *Before I go: Letters to our children about what really matters.* Lanham, MD: Sheed and Ward.

Lasagna, L. 1964. *Hippocratic oath (modern version).* Retrieved 03/10/2011.

Lehrer, J. "Are heroes born or can they be made?" The Wall Street Journal. 12/11/10.

Leo, T. "Book overdue 60 years, he pays up to make point." The Syracuse Post Standard. 09/12/06.

Liukkonen, P. and Pesonen, A. Creative Commons. recovered from kaupunginkipjasto. 10/22/2010.

MacLaskey and MacLaskey. (1920). "Is life worth living?" Clarence Darrow - Frederick Starr Debate, Garrick Theate, Chicago, IL: 03/28/20.

Malikow, M. (2010). *Being human: Philosophical reflections on psychologi-cal issues*. Lanham, MD: Rowman & Littlefield Publishing Group.

_____ (2011) "The necessity of lying." Philosophy for Business. (Electronic Journal). International Society of Philosophy. University of Shffield, UK. Issue 67. May 27, 2011.

_____ (2011). "Is it possible to be pathologically good?" Philosophy Pathways. University of Sheffield, UK. Issue 159. January 2011.

Martin, M. (1995, 1989, & 1986). *Everyday morality: An introduction to applied ethics*. Belmont, CA: Wadsworth Publishing Company.

Milgram, S. (2005). *Obedience to authority*. New York: Pinter and Martin.

Ralston, A. (2004). *Between a rock and a hard place*. New York: Atria Books.

Rand, A. (1961). *The virtue of selfishness*. New York: Penguin Books.

Rosenhan, D. (1973). "On being sane in insane places." *Science, 179*, 250-258.

Schweitzer, A. (1933). *Out of my life and thought*. Baltimore, MD: Johns Hopkins University Press.

Seligman, M. and Peterson, C. (2004). *Character strengths and virtues: A handbook and classification*. New York: Oxford University Press.

Shakespeare, W. *Hamlet*, 3.4.151.

Singer, P. (2006). "What should a billionaire give?" New York Times Magazine. 12/17/2006.

Skrocki, J. "Don't be so fast to condemn bank robbery." The Post Standard. 06/01/2009.

Strom (2003) "Doner wants to give until it hurts." *New York Times News Service*. 08/17/2003.

Szasz, T. (1973). *The second sin*. Garden City, New York: Anchor Books.

_____ (1973). *The myth of mental illness*. New York: HarperCollins.

Wallace, D. (2009). *This is water*. New York: Little, Brown, and Company.

Wheelock, C. (1910). *American education*. Volume XIV. Number 1. New York: New York Department of Education.

IV. Value Theory

Allport, G. & Odbert, H.S. (1936). "Trait names: A psycho-lexical study." *Psychological monographs: General and applied*, 47, 171-220, (1 Whole No. 211).

Baird, J. "Lowering the bar: When bad mothers give us hope. Newsweek. May 17. 2010.

Benatar,, D. (2006). *Better to have never been*. Cambridge, UK: Oxford University Press.

Coles, R. "The Disparity Between Intellect and Character." The Chronicle of Higher Education. 09/22/1995.

Gresham, J. (1988). *A time to kill*. New York: Bantam Dell/Random House, Inc.

Hoffer, E. (1983). *Truth imagined*. Titusville, NJ: Hopewell Publications.

Howard, P. (1994). *The death of common sense: How law is suffocating America*. New York: Warner Books.

Jamison, K.R. (1995). *An unquiet mind: A memoir of moods and madness.* New York: Random House.

_____. (2006). *This i believe.* New York: Henry Holt and Company.

Lafave, K.O. "Life as a human." <u>TED</u>. 03/13/2010.

Malikow, M. (2009). *Philosophy 101: A primer for the apathetic or struggling student.* Lanham, MD: University Press of America.

Mullins, A. "How my legs give me super powers." TED Conference. February 2009. Recoveredfrom http://www.quotationspage.com/ quotes/Aimee_Mullins on 05/31/2011.

O'Hara, J. "Solvay teacher admits he had sex relationship with pupil, 16." <u>The Post Standard</u>. 07/18/09.

Wicker, C. "The man sentenced to life." <u>Orlando Sentinel</u>. 05/29/89.

V. Aesthetics

Bloom, P. (2010). *How pleasure works: Why we like what we like.* New York: W.W. Norton and Company.

di Tomaso, E., Beltsano, M., and Piomelli, D. "Brain cannabinoids in chocolate." *Nature*, 08/22/1996. 677-678.

Emerson, R. (1847). "The Rhodera."

Finger, Silver, and Restrepo. (2000). *The neurobiology of taste and smell.* New York: Wiley and Liss.

Greeley, A. (1983). *A piece of my mind ... on just about everything.* Garden City, NY: Doubleday & Company, Inc.

Katen, T. (1973). *Doing philosophy*. Englewood Cliffs, NJ: Prentice-Hall, Inc.

Malikow, M. (2009). *Philosophy 101: A primer for the apathetic or struggling student*. Lanham, MD: Rowman and Littlefield Publishing Group.

_____. (2010). *Being human: Philosophical reflections on psychological issues*. Lanham, MD: Rowman and Littlefield Publishing Group.

Pascal, B. (1966). *Pensees*. Krailshemer, A. (translator). New York: Penguin Books.

Shakespeare, W. (circa 1600). "Romeo and Juliet."

Updike, J. (1989). *Self-Consciousness: Memoirs*. New York: The Ballantine Publishing Group.

VI. Metaphysics

Blood, Sweat and Tears: The Official Homepage. Recovered on 01/19/11.

Dickinson, E. (1924). *The complete poems of Emily Dickinson*. Boston: Brown, Little, and Company.

Eddy, M. (1875). *Science and health with key to the scriptures*. United States of America: The Christian Science Board of Directors.

Einstein, A. (1936). *Dear professor Einstein: Albert Einstein's letters to and from children*.

Alice Caprice, Editor. Amherst, NY: Prometheus Books.

Feeney, M. "Pulitzer prize winner is killed in accident." <u>The Boston Globe</u>. 09/29/04.

Fimrite, R. "O lucky man." <u>Sports Illustrated</u>, 10/14/1994.

Freud, S. (1916). "On transience." Berlin, Germany: Goethe Society

Hawking, S. "Briefing." Time. May 30, 2011.

Kreeft, P. (2010). *Before I go*. Lanham, MD: Rowman and Littlefield Publishing Group.

Livingston, G. (2004). *Too soon old, too late smart: Thirty true things you need to know*. New York: Marlowe and Company.

Myers, D. (2007). *Psychology*. New York: Worth Publishers.

Rubinkam, M. "Widow lived with corpses of twin, husband." Associated Press. 07/05/10.

Selzer, R. (1974). *Mortal lessons: Notes on the art of surgery*. New York: Harcourt Brace and Company.

Shakespeare, W. (circa 1600). *Hamlet*, 3.1.

Williams, M. 1986). *The veleveteen rabbit*. New York: Derrydale Books.

VII. Free Will and Responsibility

Anelli, T. "DWI prevention, not penalty." The Syracuse Post Standard. 08/14/2010.

Associated Press, "Go directly to jail; do not pass go, do not collect $20 million." 05/27/2007.

Christopher, W. (2006). *This i believe*. "A shared moment of trust." New York: Henry Holt and Company.

"A Civil Action." 1998. Touchstone Pictures and Paramount Pictures.

Clinton, W. "Briefing." Time, 03/18/2011.

Dostoevsky, F. (1997). *The gambler*. New York: W.W. Norton Company.

Jones, A. 2007. *The road he traveled: the revealing biography of M. Scott Peck*. New York: Random House.

Halgin, R. and Whitbourne, S. (2000). *Abnormal psychology: Clinical perspectives on psychological disorders*. New York: McGraw - Hill Higher Education.

Peck, S. 1995. *In search of stones*. New York: Hyperion Books.

_____. 1978. *The road less traveled. A new psychology of love, traditional values and spiritual growth*. New York: Touchstone Books.

Schlitz, D. (1978). "The Gambler." Recorded by Kenny Rogers.

Spence, G. (1996). *The making of a country lawyer*. New York: St. Martin's Press.

TPI News. Posted 03/09/2008. Recovered 05/17/2011 from www.freepublic.com/focus/f - news.